Al Roop's

View From the Stage

by

Al Roop

As told to
Adam Vaughn, Greg Cielec and Dave Hostetler

Roop Brothers Publishing
Delaware, Ohio
2017

Contributors Greg Cielec, Adam Vaughn, David Hostetler with author Al Roop

Copyrighted 2017 by Al Roop

ISBN 978-1-9767503-7-3

Second Edition, Fall 2017

Book Design, Editing and Proofreading by Dave Hostetler
Editing and Proofreading by Greg Cielec
Transcription by Laurie Irace
Art Direction and Technical Support by Adam Vaughn
Cover Design - Larry Schneeder, Delaware, Ohio
Cover Photo at Broad and Front Street, Columbus, Ohio - 4th of July, 1992

Publishing Consulting by Pink Flamingo Press and Creative Endeavors
of Cleveland, Ohio

Roop Brothers Publishing, Delaware, Ohio 2017

Yo-Yo Ma, the famous cellist, at a seminar opened his talk with what he said was an old musician joke ...

A six year old boy, sitting with his Father says to him, "Dad, when I grow up, I will be a musician."

The Father looks down at the boy, and says, "I'm sorry son, but you can't do both."

INTRODUCTION

AT A CORNER TABLE, in a dimly lit room, sits a colorful character. He is known by many in the town of Delaware, Ohio, for owning the bar with the most enviable music stage in the area. Loyal musicians aspire to play there. Loyal fans crowd the bar and its diminutive dance floor to revel in the energy of bands fortunate enough to have been booked there.

But the fellow in the corner is much more than that. He is an experienced musician in his own right and a storyteller who outshines most others in his recollection of tales from his past adventures: life on the road; a view from the stage; years of backing well-known and some not well known acts; summers of hosting a festival-quality backyard music party; and finally, bringing some of the best musicians to the intimate setting at his bar on Union Street.

Al Roop takes a shot, raises his beer and declares, "Oh, I've got some stories." He has and says, "Dozens of people have said to me, 'You've got to write this down!'"

From 1972 until the present, Al Roop has been playing music and living a musician's life. From a humble start in Columbus, Ohio, he has traveled and played shows all across the country. For years Al, and his brother Ed, who passed away in 2007, hosted the Roop Brothers Backyard Party, which drew renowned musicians, friends, and many of the area's most ardent music fans.

- Keith Flint   2014 -

PART ONE: THE EARLY DAYS

MY STORY BEGINS RIGHT HERE at the beginning, I guess. I have written down a little taste of being a drummer in various bands, beginning in the seventies. It was a life of hotel bands, six nights a week, usually a month at each hotel and then travelling to the next one. Sometimes we would have another two-week or month option — that's kind of the way it was back then. A great time! We either had Saturday or Monday off, and many times the hotel would have to have a single act come in until the full five or six piece band arrived. It was great being able to leave your equipment set up and mess around in

Al in 1954

the town. We will talk about all that later, and the travelling, some theatre shows, some of the big acts we got to open for along the way, and playing around with my brother and some of the miscellaneous craziness that it all brought on. Oh, what a life!

It definitely goes back to my mom and dad who loved music. They had friends in the nightclub business, knew some of the greatest acts, and many times had backyard parties that I was a part of for a while before I had to go to bed. I could still hear the great music that was playing on the patio, and it was a big influence in my life. There is a little break in between my sister Ginny, my brother Ed and me. We think that mom and dad only had a fun evening maybe every eight years, because my sister is now in her mid-seventies; Ed would be eight years younger than her; and I'd be eight years behind him.

I caught the good parties because they just kind of let me go, which was absolutely wonderful. They were forty years old, and my sister was just mar-

ried, and Ed was hanging out with his buddies. They would crank up the stereo, get the hor d'oeuvres and cocktails out, and they let me be a part of it.

My favorite first album had to be by Jimmy Smith. My parents played it over and over at their parties. Titled *Who's Afraid of Virginia Wolfe*, it was one of his greatest albums.

Dad and Herbie Fields

They also played the great Louis Prima and the thundering herd, who had such a shuffle groove. That's probably what taught me how to play a kick-ass shuffle and learn a good back-beat, playing along with Louie Prima albums.

I not only loved hearing those artists on the patio; but when I eventually got a set of drums, I would crank the stereo and play along with Jimmy Smith and his big grooves, as well as sax great Cannonball Adderley and his band. The song "Mercy, Mercy, Mercy," was a favorite. That's how I learned how to play, using anything I could beat on until I got drums, playing along with the bands and people I loved, which also included Wes Montgomery, Jimmy McGriff, and Groove Holmes.

I always loved the Beach Boys, and my idol, of course, was Dennis Wilson, their drummer. It might have been the *Shut Down* album that had him leaning on a 1963 Corvette Coupe, and he spoke about meeting all the girls in beautiful bikinis, playing the drums and driving his 'Vette and his XKE Jag, that created my first bucket list. Somehow I worked my way through that bucket list, and later on I was lucky enough to be involved with the Beach Boys and helping them out. It was a dream come true, which we will talk about later.

During the old parties Dad would play his cocktail drum, a long straight drum you played with brushes, along with Jimmy Smith, Chuz Alfred, and Herbie Fields, all great musicians, who would sometimes come over to our house. They would crank the stereo, and Dad would play that drum and show everybody how to play with brushes. He was quite the entertainer.

My parents loved to go to nightclubs, and they would often let me tag along. We would stop at Sandy's or some place, and they would get me a hamburger and fries. Then we would go to a nightclub, and they would put me on the inside of a booth, get me a Coca-Cola, and I would get to hear some great bands. Some of the places included the Scioto Inn on Scioto River Road in Columbus, Ohio, where Chuz played quite often; the suburban steakhouses; and Kitty's Showbar at Fifth and High, where I got to see the great Rusty Bryant's Night Train Band with Hank Marr and Jimmy Rogers playing drums; and Herbie Fields, when he would come through town from New York on his way to Miami Beach or Chicago.

Dad helped on an album Herbie recorded at their favorite club, Buddy DeLong's Kitty Showbar, an album called *A Night at Kitty's*. What a great, great album, and it is still available on the Internet. Buddy is on the cover

Dad and Chuz

with Flo the bartender. Herbie sent Dad a nice gift one day, his gold ID bracelet that he got from the Lionel Hampton Orchestra for outstanding solo on his Carnegie Hall album. Herbie was quite a decorated musician. Besides jazz, he put together an album called *Fields and Clover* with the Miami Philharmonic Orchestra. Jazz bands weren't doing stuff like that then, but he did. Then after that album he had his old soprano sax turned into a lamp and sent that to Dad, and he had his blue turquoise

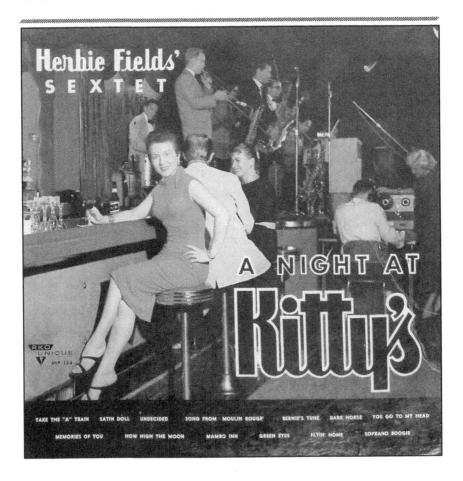

Herbie Fields' SEXTET — A NIGHT AT Kitty's

Side One

1. TAKE THE "A" TRAIN
2. SATIN DOLL
3. UNDECIDED
4. SONG FROM "MOULIN ROUGE"
5. BERNIE'S TUNE
6. DARK HORSE
7. YOU GO TO MY HEAD

(handwritten notes: "This is the first copy off the press. Thanks for everything — Barbara")

Side Two

1. MEMORIES OF YOU
2. HOW HIGH THE MOON
3. MAMBO INN
4. GREEN EYES
5. FLYING HOME
6. SOPRANO BOOGIE

✱ ✱ ✱

Personnel:

HERBIE FIELDS — Soprano, Alto, Tenor and Baritone Sax, also Clarinet. JOE BLACK — Piano. BOB DE NARDO — Guitar. LON NORMAN — Trombone. TINY MAZZA — Bass. FRANK ROOT — Drums.

✱ ✱ ✱

Production of this album was made possible by Buddy De Long of Kitty's Show Bar and Nate Roop. Original recording by Robert Buchsbaum of Coronet Recording Co., Columbus, Ohio. Cover photograph by Mike Tatom, posed by Flo Williams.

There's something about jazz that creates excitement . . . a musical excitement for both the musician as well as the listener. It's that certain "something" that makes you pat your foot or keep a finger-tapping tempo with the beat. It's as if the feeling of creating this spontaneous musical excitement is transmitted directly to the listener from the player . . . and only jazz contains such a contagious ingredient! Now . . . the trick is to capture this feeling in a recording, but with a group like HERBIE FIELDS' SEXTET providing the sounds, it's no trick at all . . . the excitement they create when they play has been captured to its fullest in this collection! You may never have strayed further West than the Jersey border, or further East than Vegas, but you'll feel like you've actually spent "A Night At Kitty's" when you spin this baker's dozen by Herbie and his swinging group!

This exciting presentation is the versatile Herbie Fields at his best. The selections range from the happy, rollicking, swinging numbers to the sweet, sentimental tunes, played for both listening and dancing pleasure. The swinging numbers are a brilliant display of Herbie's creative ability and technical skill which has made him one of the most outstanding exponents of jazz. His interpretation of melodic tunes makes you realize that Herbie Fields has a lot of sweet notes floating around in his mind which, combined with his musicianship, produce the most expressive music you have ever heard.

We cannot praise too highly, all of the members of the group. In a session like this, made up of just six pieces, everyone has to give his all. The lively trombone style of Lon Norman is outstanding, while Joe Black plays piano with incessant sweetness and feeling. Bob De Nardo's guitar work is clean and crisp. Tiny Mazza's deft fingering of the bass booms out delightfully. The steady, consistent technique of drummer Frankie Root enhances the performance.

This album is a typical grouping of the complete variety of tunes you might hear the Sextet play during one of their nightly sessions at Kitty's Show Bar in Columbus, Ohio. All of these tunes were actually recorded during one evening at the popular nightspot where the best musical groups in the country are featured, so whether or not you're lucky enough to go and hear the group in person, you can still enjoy their swing-to-sweet renditions with this on-the-spot recording. Here's your ticket to Columbus . . . and a special invitation (no cover, no minimum) for "A NIGHT AT KITTY'S" . . . HAVE FUN!

Notes by Larry Monks

RKO UNIQUE
ULP 124

Mom (left) Dad (Right) and the great drummer Buddy Rich

cufflinks made into cocktail rings for mom and her friend Nita.

***

So THAT WAS THE REAL BEGINNING. The folks ran around with some great musicians. I was probably 12 or 13 and had been asking for a set of drums, and finally got them. I had the record player to play along with and continued enjoying all of the bands mentioned earlier. It had to drive Mom and Dad crazy because as soon as I would get home from school, I would be in the basement blasting somebody and playing along.

That was pretty much the '60s, and I went through them playing along with incredible jazz bands. My first real band was called "U.S." I don't really know what the logic was behind that unless it was just for "United States." We had a big banner that was painted in black light paint with peace signs; love, not war; and a big U.S. inside of a large eyelashed eyeball. Pretty heavy stuff, but it was a good rock and roll band.

We were just basement guys for a while, and finally went out and did stuff like high school dances and the skating rink on Route 23 by the halfway house. The band was Mark Price, Lanny Partlow, Tommy Caple, Tom Coy, and myself. It was a pretty good band because we had great bands to cover back then. Grand Funk Railroad was one of our favorite bands; we did Steppenwolf's "Magic Carpet Ride"; the James Gang's "Funk 49"; a lot of Jimmy Hendrix; and Cream's classic song, "Crossroads."

Those were also the days of the great "Battle of the Bands" at the Lausche Building and the Beef and Cattle Building at the Fairgrounds in Columbus. We were never one of the great bands to play those, but one band that did was called The Tree. They later became the J.D. Blackfoot Band. The J.D. was the band that got us out to all the battles and to hear all the other bands. Years later, I would find out that one of the J.D. Band members was a favorite at Roop Brothers Bar. He was Dave Friedlander in the Mojo Kings. I went back and found pictures of the J.D. Blackfoot band to show him. They played for one of our high school parties. I made up the posters for the party and had even gone to one of their rehearsals down off East North Broadway on

Welden.

Mark Kreis has been at Roop's every Friday night for twelve years now; he also was in J.D. Blackfoot.

If we weren't in Columbus checking out J.D., we liked a band called Fire and Ice. They were kickass featuring the Nicely Brothers. The Nicely Brothers are still entertaining people to this day when they have their reunions in Delaware, but I remember going up and seeing them play under the grandstand, probably before I had a driver's license. I always liked them; they did a great version of the Doors' song "Touch Me." They could just play the hell out of it.

By now I had a driver's license, which changed everything. To this day when I tell people, "Unless you were there, people can't believe how good the music scene was back then." Any given time in the early seventies, you could go to the Sugar Shack and see Bob Seger. Nobody knew of Bob and the Silver Bullet Band yet, but for two bucks, you could go down to the Sugar Shack on campus, on 11th Avenue, and check out the Bob Seger System, a band out of Detroit that was originally Bob Seger and the Last heard. You could drive from there over to the Bistro on Olentangy River Road, just north of the OSU campus area where Kenny Rogers was playing for a two dollar coverage charge. You couldn't beat having those two guys playing in local bars.

My favorite group was a big horn band from Miami Beach with a crazy son-of-a-bitch lead singer with a big, white bouffant hairdo. I guess he was originally a trash truck driver in Miami, and his band finally caught on. They called him the White James Brown. I had heard of him, and then he started playing at the Sugar Shack. His band was called Wayne Cochran and the CC Riders. One of their famous songs was "Going Back to Miami."

The band had a killer row of horns. Wayne Cochran was nuts. He would grab a half-gallon of liquor from behind the bar and walk from table to table, still singing his ass off, while pouring people glasses full of booze. Then he would chug the rest of the bottle and throw the bottle from the dance floor up to the stage by his microphone. He would go back and get another liquor bottle and go up to the balcony and fill more peoples' glasses. Wayne Cochran and the CC Riders was just one great, hell raising, horn-blowing band.

I was making my transition from the campus bars, when my friends were still continuing to go to underage bars like the Shack, to see Pure Jam and other rock bands. We would go to local pizza places for pizza and beer, which would give us a pitcher of beer even though we were underage. My own horizons were beginning to expand.

I had learned that I could get into places that my parents took me to when I was younger. I was underage, but the Rusty Bryant Night Train Band was playing at the New Frontier on Trabue Road. I would go in ask for 151 rum and coke instead of just rum and coke. I thought that made me sound older, and they would serve me. Rusty would acknowledge me and would say, "Hi." That was cool. I'd go to the LaBoda to see Carl Sally, another incredible tenor sax player. I had severed myself from rock-n-roll and went back to the music I grew up on.

I had worked my way through the bars enough to learn that there were a lot of great acts playing at Max's Coventry Inn which became the Blarney Stone at 161 and Huntley in Columbus. There were great bands there. Eddie Pallino was one of the big bands. I went there almost nightly, still scoring underage rum and cokes. I just went with rum and coke now; I would occasionally sit in on the drums with Eddie Pallino or whomever.

One day when the Ohio State Fair was going on they were so slammed with people that Dan, the bar manager and a friend for a couple of years, knew I loved playing. He just assumed that I had to be twenty-three or twenty-four or something. He said, "Jump back here and help me bartend."

On my twenty-first birthday we had to have the party there, and Dan said, "How old are ya?"

I said, "I'm 21, finally."

He said, "You son-of-a-bitch." He couldn't believe it. It is hard to do that in this day and age, but those years being able to go into nice places underage sure paved the way for me to meet some great musicians like Donnie Wilson of the Carl Sally Band, and continuing to play with Chuz Alfred and Eddie

Pallino, who became life-long friends. I also met a man who changed my life in music, Don Beck. That's where it all changed from going to hear music, or sitting in with a band, to my first gig.

PART TWO: THE BAND YEARS, LIMO ADVENTURES, ED STORIES

IT'S PROBABLY THE SUMMER of 1973, and I worked my way into some of the great bars; got past checking out mom and dad's friends, and meeting some of my own musician friends from Max's Coventry Inn, the Ramada North, and the Sheraton North. Hotels in those days were better than any individual bar. The stage at the Ramada was behind the bar, so if you were sitting at the bar, you could see a five or six piece band doing all of the current top forty. I had discovered Studio 5 on Fifth Avenue and Marco Polo's, which had a great band called Sky King, a killer band with a girl singer. They eventually dropped the girl singer, and then people knew them as the Godz. When I started hanging out down there, it was Sky King and my good friend Don Beck at Studio 5. Luckily I worked at Imported Motor Car two blocks away on N. Star. At three in the morning I would walk there and sleep in the back of a Datsun station wagon in the show room.

Don was one hell of a guitar player and singer. He could play like anybody, incredibly fast, single-note stuff and beautiful stuff. With his pick in his mouth, he would switch to his thumb and play like Wes Montgomery and sound just like Wes. Don had a band called Amber Hue; it featured an organ player, Bob Mohney. He always had the cream of the crop in his band and did a lot of singles in the afternoons.

Bob Mohney was an incredible player back then. He was using a great rig, a Hammond B-3 organ with the bass dropped an octave and the bass coming through two fifteen-inch JBL cabinets behind him. He always had two Leslie's cabinets that have the rotary blade that spins on top. Most turned the Leslie's on with their left hand up on top of the organ. Mohney had devised a way to keep his hands on the organ. There is a volume pedal on a Hammond organ at your right foot. He put his Lesley switch on that pedal by his big toe. Instead of using his left hand, he moved his toe left, and the Leslie rotors would turn on. You would see him controlling the volume. When he wanted vibrato, his foot kicked left, and that would turn it on. He would kick left again to turn it off. The system he devised had the bass being lowered an octave, and going through the JBLs, where he kept his switch for the Leslie cabinet rotors. He came up with this for the great Jimmy McGriff.

On one of McGriff's later albums he said thanks to his first aid man, Bob Mohney, Columbus, Ohio, who fixed my organ.

Mohney had played with the Casinos when they recorded a song called "Then You Can Tell Me Good-Bye." A song from the sixties, Mohney thought it sucked, so he took $68 studio pay instead of royalty pay. The song sold millions, damn.

Don Beck was playing guitar as a studio guy and playing at the Palace Theatre and other theatres downtown. A lot of road musicians don't travel with their band; they use good local studio guys. Beck was playing with the Brecker Brothers one night and Nancy Wilson another, and a really great night with David Sanborn.

Another guy that we met at Studio 5 was a tenor sax player, Mike Flore, who became my best friend for many, many years. We played in some bands together that we will speak about later. I got really lucky and ended up in a trio with Mike playing tenor sax, Bob Mohney on organ and me playing drums. Mike had played everywhere when he went to Florida and ended up playing with the Allman Brothers and with Fat Laddy's bands. Laddy was the king of Tampa Bay area bands. Mike was in his band Rooster on and off for many years.

The other incredible guy I met was Donnie Wilson. He was the lead singer in the Carl Sally Band that featured Freddie Thomas on drums, one of the best. Donnie was on vocals and bass, and another guy that became one of my very, very best friends, Gene Deffenbaugh was on a big 335 Gibson guitar that had a beautiful, beautiful tone. He was known for what he considered "shucking," where the band would be groovin' and he would just kind of do a strumming method, dirty groove, "shucking." He could play like Wes Montgomery too, single-note player, beautiful chords and octaves.

We later had a band that I was in for many, many years, the Donnie Wilson Quartet, the DWQ. They were playing at the LaBoda, right down the road from Studio 5. The Apple Tree Lounge was down that way, along with the Suburban Steakhouse, and also the Grandview Inn.

Then I started finding out about downtown Columbus bars that were pretty hot too. We all hung around Studio 5 pretty much in the afternoon. Amber Hue, Dave Buzzards' band Caliopy, had an incredible drummer Ron Wilt in that band; and Mike Flore was the tenor sax player. Bob Mohney had switched from Don Beck's band to the new band called Gibraltar. Dave Anderson was playing sax; in fact, he played two horns at once on the song "Only You Know and I Know" by Dave Mason, and a trombone player that later joined the Ohio Players, Frank Thompson. Frank, I think, is still probably with the Ohio Players, and the drummer was Dick Smith who later went with McGuffey Lane.

We were all hanging at Studio 5 in the afternoons; and eventually, we all worked together at the Purple Jester at the Royal Inn Hotel. Bob Marvin, aka Flippo the Clown, had a bar at Reed and Henderson called the Fireside. I would say some of the popular songs back then were covers from bands like Earth, Wind and Fire; Bill Withers; Steely Dan; Traffic; Van Morrison; Chicago; Carole King; and, of course, the Doobie Brothers. We had to do all of their stuff. Another one I really loved was Boz Skaggs. I liked the song "Lowdown."

We did some Bob Seger, and by then Clapton had just come out with "I Shot the Sheriff" and boy did that kick ass. We had to do some Roberta Flack and Donnie Hathaway. Another great band we covered was the Spencer Davis Group, and I think I already mentioned Dave Mason for "Only You Know and I Know."

So as we all got more comfortable, and we were all playing the same songs, it was inevitable that the three drummers would get some harebrained idea after drinking some Schnapps in the afternoon. Peppermint Schnapps had just come out and, holy shit, was that the downfall to a lot of musicians. Anyhow, we were sitting there at Studio 5, and we thought, well, let's all go to each other's job; play the first set where we are supposed to play and when we take the break at ten o'clock go counter-clockwise to the next person's job, then on the next break, go counter-clockwise to the next person's job, without letting any of the band leaders and other band members know what was going on. We had done the first set, say at Studio 5, then I'd go to the Purple Jester and the drummer from the Purple Jester would go to Bob Marvin's Fireside Inn. The guy from the Fireside would go to Studio 5 and do that three times through the night and then go back to Studio 5 and laugh about how much fun it was.

Nobody knew three drummers were going to rotate three bands through the night, but it was all the similar songs everybody was playing and anybody could kind of intermingle, especially when you were playing with these guys, with such talented guys. I guess that's what Peppermint Schnapps will do to drummers.

***

IT WAS IN 1974 when Don Beck was at the Palace with David Sanborn doing a show downtown. Don invited David to come out afterward to hear his band at, Jim Otis' Time-Out, a fabulous nightclub. Of course, there were rules back then, dress codes. We had dress codes in the band too, but bars were really starting to have some dumb-ass dress codes. So Beck and his band Amber Hue are playing, one of the top bands in town at this new place, and he invites Sanborn to come out there. Dave comes and gets turned away at the door. The owner was kind of a nut, and they had a rule that you couldn't get into the bar with denim on. Sanborn probably had on a thousand dollar denim suit, looking like a million bucks. He was the great David Sanborn with a beautiful suit, probably had $500 Italian loafers on, but they turned him away at the door. When Beck finished the set, he wondered where in the hell Sanborn was, and he found out he had been turned away for wearing denim. What a dumbass that club owner was! It's the way the times were back then.

That was also about the time, thanks to my folks, that I lucked into a real good gig. I had mentioned Rusty Bryant and the Night Train Band. They were doing a series called Music in the Air outdoors around the city. They were at Tremont Park, Goodale Park, different parks around Columbus and Upper Arlington. The band featured Rusty Bryant on tenor sax, Bobby Pierce on organ, a guitar player Don Hales, and me. I forget who the bass player was. I was just scared to death. But my dad was thrilled I was sitting there with the incredible Rusty Bryant.

Rusty came over and stood by my side with his horn hanging over his shoulder. He just kept saying, "That's it, back beat, back beat." I just popped that snare drum. I got the snare and the rim at the same time to pop on

Rusty with Don Hales, Bobby Pierce, Larry Walters and me

shuffles drilling that back beat where you pop the end of that shuffle. Rusty was yelling and encouraging me to push the guys and that back beat makes them wail. I never forgot how to drill a swing groove, or when I got into the blues bands how important that shuffle was, that big up shuffle that you would do to bring B.B. King out. It's what you open shows with, a shuffle with that back beat.

***

SOME OF THE GREAT Columbus bars I would like to mention included one way on the west side, a supper club whose claim to fame was that they brought a little bit of Chicago and a little bit of New York right in the middle of Columbus, Ohio, LaKer's. Right down the road from it was Mother's, a bar Dave Hoon owned. It was the Town Pub for a while; I think it might have gone back to Mother's. Marco Polo's was on Fifth by Studio 5.

The Driftwood was out on the east side. Everybody called that the best place to put a band together and get paid at the same time, and Jimmy Malinkovich's Driftwood was a fun old neighborhood bar. Next to it was Pat Zell's Boathouse, another great place on the east side. Out on East Main, not far up the road was Vic Vesco's Vegas Club.

Buddy DeLong had Cerros. Buddy was the guy that had my folk's favorite bar Kitty's. Buddy was pretty cool; he gave me a pass to always get in there. The Golden Chariot, was clear out around Brice Road, and Caesars was on Main. Caesars was one of our favorite places. There was also The Purple Jester on 315, the Lincoln Lodge out on the west side and Lincoln Lanes, in Arlington, the great LaBota, Arlington Arms Imperial House; Naves Cave, the bar downstairs at Arlington Arms, the Scioto Inn, Studio 5, and the Fireside that Flippo the Clown had.

Fox and Hound Apartments had a great bar, Max's Coventry Inn, at 161. The Wine Cellar was where a lot of us played in the back bar. Another place that goes way back was the Kahiki; it had a bar downstairs that was fun to play at. Playing by the pool at the Olentangy Inn was tremendous. That's where I met The Columbus Jets, with Ottis and Bob Koker. Part of that band would later be the Mojo Kings. The Olentangy Inn, Arlington Arms, and the Lincoln Lodge were the only hotels with poolside bars and bands. I wish we still had places like that.

Probably one of the best show clubs ever, and never should have torn been down, on the eastside across the street from the Kahiki was the Desert Inn, known for the super stars of the world who played there, including all of the big bands and celebrities. The Silver Dollar on 161 was a great one. The Sheraton North and the Sheraton Downtown Sady's Stagedoor, and all of the Ramadas were great places. Some great memories, some of the favorite bars and best music were at places like the Stardust on Allegheny and the Ambassador Lounge on Allegheny.

Other places were Gordy's on Spring, a bar called My Brother's Place on East Long across the street from the Lincoln Theatre, the Needle's Eye behind Uncle Sam's Pawn Shop at Fourth and Main, and the Vogue on High Street, all fun places. Oh, the Sangrias, there was a Sangria East and a Sangria North up on Henderson. The NCO Club at the Air Base was a good one.

We played there weekly and also played on soul night. Anton's was a Restaurant in Worthington. The Valentine Family had Gordy's and the Stardust. Alvin Valentine, another great organ player and my good friend Harold Smith played at My Brother's Place on Long, wonderful people and wonderful bars.

The popular bands that we were in competition with after I eventually joined a band called Flashback, were Sweet Cheeks, Slinky and Surprise, Five Mighty People, the Bova Brothers, and Jon Pon. Another great one was George Mobley, who had the United Monster Show with Bud Fowler, The Godz, McGuffey Lane, and Black Leather Touch with my buddy Jerry Blinn and his twin brother. Oh man, killer bands.

Dave Hoon owned Mother's and had great bands like Rhodes' Brother Groove. Mickey Wilson, Eddie Pallina, the Rebounds, the Dantes, you can't forget those guys, and also Jimmy Harris' PFFT, and Dirty Billy. And, of course, Mimi Russo became a household name.

When I first met Mimi we were playing at places like the Sheraton North.

I was in Flashback, and she was in a band where she wore an evening gown and did show tunes, as well as some of the crap you had to do back then to have a good paying job six nights a week in all the popular hotel bars. Mimi was doing "Lady Sings the Blues" stuff in an evening gown, but all of a sudden a different Mimi comes out in Levis and boots in a band she called Spittin' Image. That was the band that became a household word, like McGuffey Lane. Boy, did it do her good to shit can those evening gowns and jump into tight Levis and cowboy boots because she smoked.

***

DON BECK WAS RESPONSIBLE for all of the above because he really, really fixed me up taking me under his wing. Before I was playing with bands, he always invited me to go out to my car and get my bongo drums, or sometimes I had a conga drum with me. If I didn't have anything with me, he would hand me a cowbell and always encouraged me. We later played in bands together.

He called me up one day, said he had a friend who was looking for a drummer that he could trust and wasn't a pain in the ass or have any issues. This guy had a little trio, a permanent job at the Howard Johnson's, HoJo's on 161, six nights a week. His name was Roger Hunt, and he played organ and sang. The band was the Roger Hunt Trio.

Don said that this guy Roger wanted a good personality drummer who could play anything. There was Roger and a sax player named Dave Ellis, and they both sang. It paid well, and it was a reputable hotel with a nice crowd. I knew a lot of the songs because I grew up with a lot of them. I just knew them from hearing them at my folks' house so it was easy for me to do "The Girl from Ipanema;" and of course, the great song "Night Train." Another song I loved was "Take the A-Train, It's the Fastest Way to Get to Harlem." I knew those songs by heart. We were doing jazz stuff like that, and all of the standards like "Stardust," a ballad I liked from my father, and another Latin/jazz song "Green Dolphin Street Blues." The job lasted for at least, I would say, six months or better, and by then I was really comfortable with playing out and learning different songs.

Speaking of Roger, I always thought it was interesting, that back then bands had break songs, to take each set out, and Roger had a song he particularly loved at the end of the night. I have to say it was not the highlight of what we played, but he loved to do it. It started, "And now the time has come to say goodbye, the final curtain," whatever that shit was. I just hated that damn song; it was called "My Way." So every night I knew I was about to go to the bar and have a drink because we were playing "My Way." Roger would always say, "You can remember us because I'm Roger Hunt

with an 'H.'" Boy, if the song wasn't bad enough, the Roger Hunt with an 'H' was worse. I'm sure I knew what he was thinking.

Roger was a good old boy, and I was off to the races then, playing and still going back and forth to Studio 5 and playing with those guys, but I had my own big gig. That's when Phil Traxler, who not only owned Studio 5, opened Zachariah's Red Eye Saloon. What two great bars to have; one where the gals wore evening gowns and you had the great top forty/jazz bands, and the other one with the McGuffey Lane atmosphere. That was also the year I met John Schwab. The year when I started working with Beck and the guys, he joined McGuffey Lane. Previously, McGuffey Lane had been a trio, playing everywhere, a lot at Ruby Tuesday's, I think, on Fourth Street. They decided to hire a drummer and John Schwab to make it the McGuffey Lane that most of us remember. Many times I would get off work and go down there and see

Schwab or Schwab would come over to Studio 5.

By now Donnie Wilson had known me well; he was the singer of the Carl Sally Band with the guitar player Gene Deffenbaugh. Our paths had crossed a lot; and they knew I was playing full-time, and it was working out. They were also looking to leave Carl Sally and hire a gal named Vicki Travis, a beautiful woman with a great voice. They wanted to leave the jazz thing they were doing and go into top forty and soul with me, Vicki, Gene playing guitar, and Donnie Wilson playing bass. Plus all three had great vocals. They may have asked Beck where to find a drummer, and I left the Roger Hunt Band to join that band because that was just a dream come true to be doing cool soul and the neat side of top forty stuff with the great Donnie Wilson and Gene Deffenbaugh. We stayed together and traveled all over for years.

Gene unfortunately passed, but, oh my gosh, did we have fun. We later had a couple different guitar players, and Donnie and I stayed together playing from time to time for many, many years. I would say up until the nineties.

***

AT THIS POINT I'M a full-fledged playing son of a bitch, I thought. There was nothing else I wanted to do besides cruise from gig to gig, and if I wasn't playing I was out sitting in with one of the other guys or checking out another band. My life had a great beginning with these guys. You know they were the cream of the crop back then, and I was so lucky to meet them and so lucky they liked me, guys like Don Beck, Bob Mohney, Mike Flore, Gene Deffenbaugh, and Donnie Wilson. I was very lucky for a young drummer to be playing with these badasses. I don't think I even realized what

badasses they were, at the professional levels or where they were in their lives, and who their friends were.

The Donnie Wilson Band, what a great band that was, was one of the most beautiful times in my life. It's pretty hard to believe, just great, great songs, with a great band. Gene was my very best friend. At the time he lived out on Georgesville Road in an apartment. I spent a great deal of time out there, and then later he moved in with his girlfriend in German Village at Kossif and Mohawk, right across the street from the Mohawk Grill. A brick house, I spent a lot of time living there with those guys. My father grew up in that area; he spoke about the hill at Schiller Park and riding sleds there; and I was able to tell Dad I beat him on that one. I didn't ride a sled on Schiller Park hill, but I did christen the top of the hill early one morning. I think that got a little smile out of him.

Some of the songs we did were absolutely the best you could do if you loved old soul. We were doing stuff like Major Harris' "Love Won't Let Me Wait." Our break song was "Mister Magic" by Grover Washington. Donnie did his signature song, "I Stand Accused" by Jerry Butler. When Donnie would sing that song waitresses would come up on stage and wipe his brow off. He had great dynamics; he would be singing and when it came to the right time, he would belt out this scream that just fit perfectly and bring the volume down, so much soul, then the band would continue on and build up again to his next controlled scream. It was something.

Some of my other favorites were all of the Sam and Dave stuff, like "Hold On, I'm Coming"; another signature Donnie Wilson song was "On Broadway"; and we also did some James Brown stuff, and some Isley Brothers, Isaac Hayes and Curtis Mayfield.

My sister's favorite song in the whole world is "Proud Mary." So many times if Ginny came in, whatever band I was in, we would play "Proud Mary" for her. But the Donnie Wilson Band version was the best. We funked it up, it started normal, but after the head of the song, it pulled back and turned funk. Then it turned into Sly and the Family Stone's "Dance To The Music."

The Donny Wilson Quartet - Al, Donny, Vickie and Gene

We did a James Brown medley of "Lick 'em Stick" and "Little Groove Thing." It had a break, to see if I could count, as Donnie would say. He would bring the song down low and say it's going to get tricky, and yell, "Are you ready drummer? I want you to give it to me one time one time." I'd hit once then a four beat fill, back to the groove, then Donnie would say, "Give it to me two times." I'd hit my drum two times and a four beat fill, back to the groove, let's try three times one time, I'd do it and back to the groove, Donnie would say, "It's getting harder, are you listening drummer?" I'd yell back, and then he'd say, "I want you to give it to me four times, two times, one time then take it to the bridge." Bap bap bap bap, four bear fill, then bap bap bap bap, four beat fill, then it went up a step, and to the bridge. I'd go up on the bell of the cymbal and push that big James Brown funky groove.

We were doing Sheraton jobs, working at the Sheraton North; and after the bar closed and everybody left, we would go back in and rehearse new songs. Back then whatever new top forty was out, you had to learn a new one every two weeks, sometimes one a week to stay really current. We would go down at three in the morning and figure out a couple tunes and work on them, and then present them the next night.

One night we went back to the hotel room, probably about five in the morning, and Donnie goes, "Oh boy, man aren't you hungry?" He had a plan. He went down to the hotel lobby and said, "I left my guitar case and my guitar in the bar." Actually he walked back to the hotel room with his guitar, but his case was at the bar. They let him in, and he got his guitar case and was walking through the kitchen to get back out, and he saw the bacon they fried for the morning. They pre-baked tons of bacon. He must have put two pounds of bacon into his guitar case with a loaf of bread, and a cherry pie he spotted that they baked for the next day.

He came back to the room, where we were all starving, and all we had were some beers there in the cooler. He opened up that guitar case and said, "Look at this." Boy, we were all dying for a bacon sandwich. And then he said, "Well, I got my little brother here." He pulled his switchblade out, and cut the pie up for us all. That was a beautiful evening.

When I played in The Donnie Wilson Band, we had a hit with a stunt we came up with when we played at Arlington Arms Imperial House, in the bar downstairs, Nave's Cave, which was run by Lee Begin, a huge Buckeye fan. He always bought us Buck-

eye clothes. Lee and I would see who could blow the biggest ball of fire before Buckeye games, putting 151 in our mouths, then spitting out and lighting it in a big fireball. Another good one was when we were working at the Sheraton going towards Wheeling, West Virginia in St. Clairsville. It was up on a hill, out where they built a big mall, and we were out there quite a bit, for two weeks or a month at a time. At the time we opened the second set with a Santana song, "Evil Ways." While the stage lights were still off, I would put some 151 rum on my snare drum and light it on fire. I would use my mallets and go around the drums splashing fire, then into the song. By then the rum would usually burn off and it was a neat fiery beginning to "Evil Ways." But I had put too much rum on my snare drum and the fire didn't go out, and it got on the carpet. I was trying to put it out with my feet and still trying to play the song, and it got back into the red velvet drapes behind me.

We are in this beautiful room, and my drums were on fire, the carpet a little bit, and the drapes a little bit, so we finally had to quit playing the song and get the fire under control. To our surprise, or not to our surprise, they didn't think they needed us any longer after that night.

I remember Gene saying, "Well, we're booked here for the week of New Year's Eve and New Year's Eve night, how's that working?" And they were nice to explain that that wasn't working well. That was a little set back, but in the meanwhile while we were there, we met a band down the road at the Holiday Inn, called JJ, that featured someone who would later be my good friend, Jerry Ambrosini, and a girl, Dale Krantz. She would eventually marry Gary Rossington of the Rossington Collins Band. To this day Dale is still with Gary, and is leader of the backup singers in Lynyrd Skynyrd. We all had quite a good time.

I have never been known to say girl, gal, lady or chick. I once took a job at the State Fair and said I had previously worked in a trio with a 'chick' singer, and Juice Newton gave me hell, saying, "That's a 'lady'."

The road was pretty wild for Donnie, Gene and me. Another great one was at the Sheraton Patriot in Virginia. They had a real shithead manager, I mean, he was just a little arrogant prick. He said over, and over, "There is no partying, no drinking, and don't socialize with the staff. I want nothing going on in your rooms because you are just here to perform and don't do anything wrong."

Oddly enough, some friends of ours were playing in a show club down the road, maybe an hour or two away. Crazy buddy Ron Wilt and the show band he was in showed up, and we were not supposed to have any parties or party with the staff, but we had the bartenders and some waitresses and this other band in our room. We had a hell of an opening night or second night, whatever it was.

The next night there was a different band setting up in there, and we asked what was going on. The manager said, "Fuck you. I told you no fraternizing with the staff and no partying in your rooms." We did have a pretty good party, but we didn't know our friends from Columbus from another show band were going to show up, hell, it wasn't our fault. Anyhow, they thought they would let us go. We knew our buddies only had that one night off; and since we didn't have anything to do the next day, we drove down to the ocean or wherever they were and walked in on them. They didn't know that we had been fired. We thought we would return the favor, drink with them and try to get them fired. Holy shit, that was good one.

We also ran into each other in Jekyll Island, Georgia, and that time I was with my buddy Jerry Ambrosini. There was a very cool food and beverage manager there and nobody lost his job.

Life with Donnie and Gene was something. Gene and I would work at the air base at the NCO club, which we loved, and going back to Gene's place on the westside there was a putt-putt golf course that had three courses. After midnight you could play all of them as long as you wanted for the price of one. Gene would set his bottle of JTS Brown whiskey outside the fence, by the pop machine, and we would buy some cokes and pour them out a little for the JTS Brown and play golf into the night.

Donnie and I would end up in a trio with Bob Mohney at Sady's Stage Door downtown Columbus at the Sheraton. It was in the early eighties and different for us. Mohney was playing a grand piano, Donnie bass and vocals, and me. It was very cool.

***

I AM OFTEN ASKED what are my all time favorite bands. It's always been the Tower of Power, the Allman Brothers, James Brown, Albert Collins, the Blues Brothers, and, of course, the Beach Boys. My favorite drummer from 1974 until today is David Garibaldi of the Tower of Power. They started in 1968 in Oakland, California. Dave left them for a bit, but he's back with them to this day. The Tower of Power really made funk, super funk. Dave is master of ghost notes (beats that you leave out) and a sync caped groove.

My favorite bass player in the world is Francis "Rocco" Prestia of the Tower of Power; he is the best in the world. Nobody can come anywhere near the imagination of Rocco, and Rocco with Dave is the most kick-ass rhythm section. Another one of my favorite bass players would not be a string bass player, but an organ bass, that they play with their left hand, sometimes their left foot, like Jimmy Smith, and his big Hammond B-3 organ.

***

I REMEMBER A NIGHT at the Top of the Center at Third and East Broad. I was with my buddy Ron Wilt, drummer from Caliope at the time, and another drummer Ralph, who was playing at the Top of the Center at the Sheraton. You had three drummers together, drinking, and that's bad. Everybody was sitting at a table. It was a beautiful room, and there were people there for dinner. It was one of the first bars that looked out over Columbus, and always had a sophisticated band with good players. But Ralph had that crazy girl with him and she didn't quite fit with the rest of us. She took it a little too far, she could only talk about the butterflies landing on the wing; how beautiful the bees were; and talk of trees. She decided that we were all pretty out of control and that she should recite poetry. Well, that was it, and apparently it even bored the rest of the room, because they loved the outcome. Ol' Ralph stood up and said, "I got a poem for you...

Hooping and a dooping.
The door flew open.
In walked Frankenstein.
He said to his bitch with the seven-year itch,
'Baby your pussy's mine.'
Out in the kitchen mammie was bitching,
knocking dickheads with a spoon.
The fuck was so thick it made Dracula sick,
and the Count jumped over the moon. Ralph, 69."

She stood up, grabbed her purse, got her car keys out, and stormed off. Six or seven tables around us stood up and applauded as she walked out of the room.

Another one I had to love with these dumbasses who were great musicians at Studio 5 one night and I was playing and looking over at Bob Mohney playing organ. He was dating one of the most beautiful girls, Jane, who waitressed there. She walked right in front of the stage with a tray of drinks, looked over at Bob and smiled at him. She was gorgeous. Bob looked over at me and acted like he was spitting something out and picking his teeth. I knew what he meant, like he had something stuck between his teeth. I thought, damn, you lucky son of a bitch.

Not long after that a gal walks in the door, past the coat-check girls, and comes around over to the front of the stage with a little dog. I think it might have been a Cocker Spaniel. She ties the dog up to the leg of Bob's organ and leaves a suitcase and storms off. Bob looked over at me again without quite such a happy smile, as it was his soon to be ex-wife tying his dog up to the organ and leaving his clothes. He said, "God-damn, and the dog needs an operation."

That all happened within a half-hour. Ah, you can't put a price on shit like that. The good and the bad. He had a good moment, and then it all turned to shit.

We were going to the old Grandview Inn, across from the Laboda, in the Upper Arlington area, where they used to have some players like the incredible trumpet player, Maynard Ferguson. He was well known for his version of "MacArthur's Park," but he did some other cooler shit. And that made me think of the day when I was just a kid, back when I was still underage, and how I went to Scott's Inn, up on Sinclair Road, because Lou Rawls was there.

I had a suit on and everything; so they let me in, and I sat at a table with a business-looking guy, and I got the chance to check out Lou. I always liked Lou Rawls, and he signed a napkin for me before he left. I'll never forget it. Lou thanked me for coming in and signed the napkin, "To Al, have a ball, soulfully, Lou Rawls."

***

BACK IN THE SEVENTIES bands had to go through a lot of red tape. Holy crap. There was a union, and everybody had to comply or you would get blackballed from a bar or blackballed from the union. There always had to be a designated bandleader. You had to file a contract if you were at the Sheraton or the Sangaria, or anywhere you were, and you had to do a contract for Local 104, Columbus Federation of Musicians.

It was something. We all thought it was shit, but we had to pay it. They would come in bars; and if they found a musician in the band who's dues weren't up to date, they would charge him one hundred bucks and the leader of the band a hundred fifty bucks. Of course, the leader made the musician pay both of them because it wasn't his fault.

And when you did contracts, you had to fill out a contract for $2950 for the union to be legal; but then you re-write one for $2500 for the bar for what you were really going to get for the week. Back then we were normally doing five or six nights a week, and bands were doing great. Hell, we were making five hundred bucks a piece a week. No expenses and five hundred dollars. But when we played out of town, we had to take 10% off the top for their union because we were in their musicians' bread and butter area. So, if we played in Indy, they got 10% off the top.

The contracts and the blacklist shit were pretty crazy. The Columbus Federation of Musicians is gone now, but they used to send a monthly booklet out, and embarrass everybody that was blacklisted. What was really funny was that I kept my card in my wallet, and I bet the last time I paid my dues, by quarter, was in 1978. But I kept my card.

***

DAVE HOON HAD the Town Pub. Dave's a great guitar player and singer. He took care of us musicians. He was a great brother musician and fellow bar owner. He had some bars downtown. Ron Wilt, the drummer from Caliopy, got me in other shit. He was sitting there with John Hicks, a big OSU football player who had his big brown Lincoln Mark IV sitting out in front.

There was John, Dave, Ron, and me. That's when Schnapps came out. We were being stupid, hanging out. I think I was on a roll because I played there the night before. As my memory works, I stayed there all-night and slept underneath the pool table, on my coat.

I woke up and at eleven a.m. all of the regulars were coming in. Back then car phones were very big and cumbersome, and they sat on the hump on the floor of the car. Ron Wilt, the drummer, said to me, "Al, go up to that brown Lincoln. The phone's going to ring in a minute."

I went out and opened the passenger door. I was looking at the phone on the hump of the car, a big ass phone, waiting for it to ring. All of a sudden this enormous black hand fills the window of the car and the guy says, "What are you doing?"

"I'm waiting for the phone to ring," I said innocently.

"The phone is not going to ring," he says, and he pulls me out and closes the door. We went back inside; they were all dying laughing. They told big John Hicks, football player, that some little skinny white guy was out there trying to break into his Lincoln. I probably only weighed one hundred fifty pounds then, and here it looks like I am breaking into big John Hicks' car, and he came out to handle it. I was still learning the game of hanging with the big boys.

Every so often bands liked to switch up, as great as the situation you were in sometimes it's time to change. Bob Mohney, Mike Flore and myself were at Studio 5, and we were talking about a new job that just the three of us could do that would not require any rehearsing. We could play any standard, and we could play any of the top 40. We were even doing a hot version of "2001 Space Odyssey," all funked-up.

***

WE HEARD THERE WAS a new bar out on the far westside of Columbus, out near New Rome, past the Lincoln Lodge. It was a show club, LaKer's Super Club. It was quite the place. They had the show side for nice dinners, a lobby with a coat check girl, and the other side lead into a nice nightclub where they needed an act.

Mike and I left Studio 5 and went out there to see the manager about a gig. We told him we had been together for years and years. Of course, we had never been together as a trio ever, but we told him we even had clothes that match. He said, "Well, what's the name of the band?"

We looked at each other. I didn't know what to say, and Mike always looks like he has a buzz, but he managed to say, "It's High Street."

The manager said, "Well what, High Street Show, High Street Review?"

Mike said, "It's the High Street Trio." Sure enough he gave us the job full time. We started the next week, and it was a six night a week job. We had beautiful signs all hand painted on the wall, now featuring the fabulous High Street Trio.

I asked Mike, "How in the hell did you pull 'High Street' out of your ass?"

It was a neat club, and Lou, the manager, took good care of us. Some of the bands that played in the big room included The Platters; they were there for a week. It was great to check them out. And from the Jackie Gleason Show, Frank Fontaine, did a skit at a bar on the Jackie Gleason show where he was Crazy Guggenheim, "Hi ya, Joe." A great skit. And a fabulous singer Johnny Desmond was there.

A lot of times I would stay at the hotel right down the road. It was pretty inexpensive, and during the day they had a real nice bar right beside the pool, outside on a patio under a roof and cabanas. A lot of times I would get a little one-bed cabana there and enjoy the evening. One morning, Johnny Desmond was sitting out there having a screwdriver and enjoying himself. That's where LaKer's put up those guys; one time I sat with Frank Fontaine. That was pretty cool. They also had another band, The Williams' Family Show, from Arkansas. They had an 8-piece band; it was all family, and their daughter was pretty cute as was their drummer. So a lot of times they would come in and watch us.

Mohney thought their bass guitar player was pretty good, and he would come into the lounge to see us play. Bob had just his kick-ass Hammond B-3 bass lines. I would look over; Bob was smiling, and he switched his hands. Instead of playing lead with his right and bass with his left, he was playing the bass lines backwards with his right, and his left hand crossed-over playing lead, just to blow the guy's mind a little bit. It was amazing the stuff Mohney could do.

One time at some other bar we were cranking and Mohney had it going on. He may have had a little buzz, which was rare for him. Bob's a good-looking guy, but he had a pretty good size beak on him. He had real long hair, a bunch of turquoise, a trimmed-down beard, and that nose. I looked over, and he was looking at me and Flore, and he bent over and started playing a

La-Ker's

BY
DIVEN CARLILE

Two new groups came to La-Ker's Supper Club last Monday night. The Williams Family will be appearing in the main dining room six nights a week through the 29th of this month. This family group, featuring song medleys stretching from the roaring twenties to toned down glitter rock, is all show-biz; their act a curious mix-ture of serious music and slap-stick comedy.

In La-Ker's lounge owner Lewis Kerr has landed a group with threatens to make his club a mecca for serious music lovers in this city. The High Street Trio with Bob Mohney on organ, Mike Flore on sax and drummer Al Roop is a group of serious musical ability, refreshing in a town where such talent is often hard to find.

Their style of jazz is in-tricate but accessable, mellow but exciting in its clarity and improvizational creativity.

The expertise of these men on the instruments they play so well was, in short, a pleasant surprise.

Fantastic
The "HIGH ST."
♭♭ TRIO
OPENING March 17th

hell of his organ solo with his nose! Still playing bass with his left hand, he knocked out a good solo and then swiped his nose across the keys, just like you would normally with your hand at the end of your solo.

I remember when we started at LaKer's we had

to get shirts. We told him that we had clothes. We all had white pants or black pants from other bands. We went to Silverman's and bought a couple of matching strange silk shirts so we always looked alike, and we got away with it. One night, Lou was up at the Lincoln Lodge on a Friday or a Saturday night listening to their band. I played there a lot with the Donnie Wilson Band and knew some people there. Lou said, "I want you to come down here and play."

I said, "Well, that's not right. We can't do that. We don't know their equipment, and we're not invited."

He said, "You are invited. It's my bar and I want you to leave there now. I paid these guys for their equipment for the rest of the night. I tipped them well, and you are invited to come down and play their stuff so get your ass down here."

This has never happened – ever again. We go down there, and they buy us some drinks, and the guys show us the organ and the drums. Mike had his sax with him, and we did the set. Lou got to hear his favorite band there.

I loved the Lincoln Lodge with cabanas by the pool and the bar. It had a circle driveway around the front of the hotel, in the middle it had a putt putt area, a big circle with five or six holes with flags. We would go over there and play putt putt sometimes. One night it led into shooting pool with the golf clubs held backwards. It was pretty late, and all of the guys thought that would be funny to leave me there. I was taking a little nap with my club by the hole; I don't know if I made the shot or not. When I woke up, the grass was dewy; I knew I had been had once again.

The owner of the LaKer's wanted us to be on the Bob Braun Show, a noon hour TV show in Cincinnati called the 50-50 Club. The owner just scared the hell out of Bob. He was afraid he was going to break his fingers if we didn't do it, and we didn't. Instead we went to Denver.

***

BOB KNEW SOME PEOPLE in Denver with a hot show band called The Sparklers. We thought we would move out there and say the hell with the LaKer gig, and we did oddly enough. We rehearsed with a couple of bands and tried to make a stay of it. It was great when we had a job. You had a hotel room, and then we would have a couple of weeks off. He knew some people so he was staying with them, but I was living in my van in hotel parking lots, so I had a nice bathroom at whatever hotel I could find. Sometimes I had a place to shower and clean up, like at the Royal Inns. I got up one day and there was about two foot of snow on the ground; it had been sixty or seventy degrees the day before. But it was an experience; a lot of people told me that I would probably get stranded, that shit doesn't work out too good sometimes.

You can't get another job to help out if you don't have a Denver license, and if you don't have your car inspected and, and all kinds of shit repaired, you can't get a license, and you can't get another job. If you are not playing for a couple of weeks, you are kind of up shit creek. But I made do, I had some beer, some bread, peanut butter and butter in my little fridge in the back of the van. It was carpeted and laid out pretty good so I just hung out.

During the day I would drive up to Golden, Colorado, to the Coor's Brewery and take the tour, because you knew it ended up in the hospitality room where there was free beers. Oddly enough one of the tour guys was Randy Gradishar, an Ohio State Buckeye who was out there. He eventually was with the Denver Broncos, and he would always take the two-beer limit off for me. Another group of people would come through, and he would usually say, "Al, do you want another one?" and that was how I occupied my days. Sometimes he would come out to Turn of the Century bar to see us.

One of the things you did in the Coors tour when you are walking from one building over to another, you crossed over a covered bridge with windows over maybe six or eight rows of box cars. They would stop there and look out the window and the tour guide would say, "Okay, here's one for you, now those box cars down there, how many cases of Coor's beer would you suppose you could get in a box car?"

Somebody would say, "A million."

He would go, "How about you, ma'am?"

And she might say, "Twenty-seven hundred."

He looked over at me, and I knew what the number was, I knew it exact, I said, "48,400."

He said, "Well, Sir, you are right, and you have taken the tour too many times." He was kind of teasing me, then he pulled me aside later, and he said, "Just take the short tour. That's what the kids from the Colorado School of Mines do. You can come up and get a pass and go right in the exit door into the hospitality room, and drink your two beers." Knowing Randy, I was able to drink as many as I wanted. Then I would take a nap and life would go on.

***

I EVENTUALLY HAD TO make my way back home. The job ran out, and the peanut butter and Coors ran out. Gas money was just about history. Going through Nebraska and Iowa just sucked. There is no more god-awful place in the world then Nebraska, where it is like driving through a burnt flat field for a day.

When I got over into Des Moines, Iowa, I saw a Royal Inn Hotel there, and I knew the Royal Inn from playing at the Purple Jester Bar at the Royal Inn on Olentangy River Road. I thought they will probably have a cocktail hour with chicken wings and all of the goodies, a pool and a nice bathroom by the pool with a shower. I put my suit on in the van and went in and swam a little bit, took a shower, cleaned-up, and dried my hair. I went out to the van, put a change of clothes on, and by then it was four or five p.m. Sure enough, cocktail hour was going on, and they were going to bring out the hors d'oeuvres. I didn't have a penny. But I kept going, putting it on a tab. I must of stuck out with my long hair and beard, and my Levis or whatever, because when the band came in, they even asked, "Are you a player?"

And I said, "Yes." I did nothing that I should be proud of, but I was just desperate and bored, and I had been living in that van for a while. I was taking advantage of the buffet, drinking shots and beers, and I told them I was indeed in a band on my way to Chicago, just staying there for the night and having some fun. I won't even mention the band I said I was in, but it was a real good one. I got a round of drinks for the band and took them up on a tray.

I think I did that again and they said, "We would like to thank so and so, the drummer from the blah, blah band; he's hanging out with us tonight; maybe we will get him up here to play something."

Meanwhile the tab for the buffet and the drinks was mounting up. A buddy of mine, a musician who had a hard time getting away from people, would order a pack of cigarettes and a beer when he was going to "Houdini" on them. Actually, it was Mohney; he paid his bill; he just couldn't say bye. Nobody ever leaves a pack of cigarettes was the scheme. I was getting scared about the money. So I said, "Oh, I will have another beer and a pack of Marlboro Reds. I will be right back."

And they said, "Well, sure Al."

I went out past the pool got in my truck and got the hell out of there as fast as I could, down the road to another hotel, pulled around the back and slept it off. Coming home the next morning, I needed to get over a toll bridge. I had Mohney's nice bike helmet. He took a dirt bike out with him, and somehow I ended up with his helmet. Maybe he rode it to a job one night and put it in my van. But I thought well, hell, he isn't here. And the guy said, "We don't need a helmet in this state, but we will give you enough money for gas and get you across that bridge."

I sold a base pedal. I think I took ten bucks for it. That got me home, but that was a good trip. I probably went right back with the Donnie Wilson Band. In fact, I am sure I did. We did that several times.

***

IT'S TIME FOR AN ED STORY. This isn't the best one, but it was sure a time in my life when I got to do something you don't ever get to do. Ed called me and said he had a great deal. He went to school with the guy who owned Columbus Fireworks, and he was always helping out at the Upper Arlington Fourth of July Fireworks. He said they needed another guy to help out with the fireworks show over at the Park of Roses, off High Street. I said oh, hell, I would love to do that. I was supposed to play at Howard Johnson's that night. I told HoJo the offer I had, they didn't know if they were going to stay open very long anyway. They were dead. So I went ahead and went down to the fireworks.

As I was pulling in, people were lined up along the driveway clear to the back of the Park of Roses. I heard somebody say, "He must be one of the lighters," or something like that, and I thought this is cool as hell.

Back then fireworks were not electronically shot. They had the two different size mortars in the ground, and the fireworks were laid out carefully; big shells wrapped in brown paper, and they had a big wick coming out. Each were lit with flares.

My job was to keep the tarp over them. I would lift the tarp up and the guy would select what to stick in the mortars, then I'd cover up the shells and a guy would ignite them. It just seemed amazing that my brother and I were doing major fireworks there at the Park of Roses and in Upper Arlington.

That led to many years down the road when we still had a connection with those guys. That's how we were able to go up to Columbus Fireworks and rent a couple of mortars and buy a bunch of the fireworks for one of the Roop Brothers parties. I actually got to see the gold spider, one of my favorite fireworks, fill the sky over my house. We really pushed this too far that night. One shell came out of a bigger mortar, it got up near the top, and blew the top eight or ten inches off this half inch thick steel, five inch in diameter mortar. We found it over the roof in the backyard of the house across the street the next day. We thought we had better quit the firework shit before we killed somebody. Ed did bust an eardrum.

***

OF COURSE, STUDIO 5 was the meeting spot again. It was either Studio 5 or Marco Polo's, one of the two. Upper Arlington was going strong, so it was probably Marco Polo's. I was flying down there from Clintonville. I was coming down North Star, just north of Lane Avenue, there is an "S" turn on North Star that had the OSU cow pasture to the east and houses to the west. I thought I had it just fine, storming through that curve, but that wasn't true.

The ass-end of the car went out through the farm fence into the OSU cowfield, that fortunately didn't have cows in it any longer. The police came when we had it about "doctored" up. The policeman was asking me questions and I said, "My brother-in-law is Phil White." Phil was an Arlington policeman at the time, and everybody loved Phil, everybody. I was sitting in the back with the clipboard. The steering wheel cut my little finger a little bit, but it just took some skin off. I was smearing-up the paperwork on the clipboard.

The policeman then said, "Just give me that back. This one is on Phil. But you get your ass back here tomorrow and replace those fence posts with some that aren't bent or me and Phil will have your ass."

I said, "Certainly!" and got out of that somehow, and we got down the road. It's a wonder I didn't go to jail; it was the mid-early seventies, but thank God for my brother-in-law and everybody loving him.

***

AS ALWAYS, I ENDED up back with the Donnie Wilson Band. Sometimes we called it "DWQ", the Donnie Wilson Quartet. It was a good band.
I mentioned earlier that we played in St. Clairsville, Ohio, and down the road at the Holiday Inn was a band called "JJ." One of my best friends to this day, Jerry Ambrosini, who lived in Fort Wayne at the time, was in the band.

It turns out the band JJ's drummer was leaving, and they considered me as a replacement. They were playing at the Holiday Inn Solar Dome in Fort Mitchell, Kentucky. That was when they first started covering the center of Holiday Inns, covering the pools and making it a big courtyard. They had tremendous bars in the solar domes.

So after work at Arlington Arms, I would drive clear to Fort Mitchell, which was actually the Cincinnati area, and hung out with them and talk about what we were going to do. That's how I joined the band. I went down four or five times. I had given my band a two-week notice again, and they didn't have a problem finding another drummer.

I wanted to join these guys. Jerry, the guitar player, had a beautiful black 335 Gibson "Sally." He would even take the Sally into Denny's Restaurant with us to eat. He never left her in the car. They were doing some Rufus and Pointer Sisters, and a great job on the Doobie Brothers. Dale, the gal singer, did a hell of a job on "Only Women Bleed." Not too many bands were pushing the envelope like we were. And I really liked the version she did of "You're the Best Thing – you're the best thing that ever happened to me." We also did Ambrosia's "Holdin' On To Yesterday." What a beautiful song! Between Jerry's guitar and Dale's voice, it was kick-ass. So, that's how I ended up in the band JJ.

***

BY THE TIME I was leaving the Donnie Wilson Band, JJ was going to Ocala, Florida. Later Dale got offered to do another job that she couldn't turn down. With her leaving the band, the agent didn't want to continue on, but Jerry and myself, and the keyboard player, Jim Derazio, decided to continue looking for work in Florida.

We were staying at my Grandfather's vacation place around Lake Wales. I knew where the key was. After awhile in Central Florida, Jim decided to go back to Pennsylvania.

It was kind of neat looking at our license plates – there was one from

Ohio, one from Indiana, and one from Pennsylvania. So it ended up just me and Jerry. We went on to Fort Lauderdale to see what would happen there. We had some awfully good times at this one place, Mr. Pat's, which was a pretty well known nightclub. It was part of a restaurant called Pat's Starbucks Steakhouse. Like everything was back then, Pat's was a fancy joint. If you didn't have a collared-shirt, there was one on the rack you could go put on

Dale Krantz

and get into the place and enjoy the show bands.

The guy's name running the place was Louie. He had a meeting with us, and he liked us, so we were hired to start the next week. He said, "Get in here Monday, and we will get that haircut, and get those beards trimmed up, and get you fitted for the right clothes. Go out and see Big Tommy at the bar, and you will be taken care of the rest of the night. Welcome to the crew."

We went out and saw Big Tommy and here was a beautiful gal, a big gal, in a tuxedo. She said she heard we were sent out, and we were being comped. So we drank everything we possibly could, ate good, and crashed in my van instead of getting a hotel room. We got up the next day and Jerry said, "He's out of his damn mind. We are not cutting our hair, and not wearing those fruity clothes. Let's get the hell out of here."

So we decided to head for Clearwater Beach, and it was a good choice. There

Me & Jerry Ambosini at Clearwater Beach

were a lot of good players over there. Musicians have always hung out in the bay area, that's what they call the Tampa/St. Pete/Clearwater area; it was a great time, and we never forgot it. Jerry met his wife Debbie when he moved to San Francisco, and they just recently moved out of California to St. Augustine, Florida.

We ended up coming back from Florida in probably one of the worst snowstorms ever. North of Cincinnati Jerry waved to go up I-75, toward Fort Wayne, and I went up I-71 toward Columbus. I remember the snowstorm was so bad the windshield wipers iced up and one of them flew off because it was so dam heavy. But I ended up coming back to the old Lincoln Lodge and getting a room for the night and getting home the next day.

The next thing I did was rejoin the Donnie Wilson Band. We lost the great guitar player and friend Gene Deffenbaugh, so we called Jerry who was still in Fort Wayne, and we played every Friday and Saturday in Columbus. Jerry would come in from Fort Wayne and spend the weekend. We did that for probably six months off and on. Jerry became the new lead guitar player for the Donnie Wilson Band.

***

WHILE WE ARE STILL in the mid-seventies, another Ed story. Ed and I were a little different in age, eight years. He worked at the Zoo Bar, a place in

Grandview on Fifth Avenue. While at the Zoo, the character he was, after he had heard of something I did, he told me his adventure of seven or eight years earlier. He decided to go in the front door of the Zoo Bar and out the back door on his Triumph motorcycle. Everyone laughed their asses off about it. So, this was probably in 1974. Phil Traxler, the wild man that owned Studio 5, had an idea for me. The odd thing is my brother did this on a bike at the Zoo Bar, and they talked me into doing it on a motorcycle-looking mini-bike at Studio 5. The Zoo and Studio 5 were the same bar, very little change other than the name. I was out in Traxler's Suburban, he cracked a bottle of Lancer's Wine and said, "Well, let's drink this." He then said, "What we want you to do is take all of your clothes off." A guy was outside revving up the little mini-bike.

I said, "Are you out of your mind?"

He said, "Just drink the wine." I drank the wine and streaking was the rage back then. I thought a lot of Traxler, so I ended up taking off my clothes after we finished the bottle of Lancer's. I stepped out onto the bike and headed for the door of this beautiful place, full of cozy areas facing the bandstand, with couches, lava lamps and paper ball lamps, it was pretty cool. There was a couple that had just crossed the street, well dressed, leaving Studio 5, hand-in-hand. I happened to look at them when I was getting on the damn mini-bike and heading for the door. I got through the door and past the coat-check girl, who sees me and her hair is almost sticking straight up. I swung to the right and then an immediate left over the dance floor, shooting past the band. I think it was Beck's band, Amber Hue, and they were just in hysterics laughing. I went around the corner to the left and then faced the bar. I've got a picture somebody took of me, after I had just passed Mimi, a server there.

I remember catching the wall in the front, I did a zig-zag to get out, and I pushed myself off the wall and got outside threw the damn mini-bike down and got into that Suburban again and we were toasting with more wine. I looked across the street, and the couple that were holding hands before I went in the bar were in exactly the same spot, still holding hands, like they

Mimi cracks up as I barrel past her naked on a mini bike. That's me to the left.

saw a ghost. I'm sure they were shocked.

What are the chances of two brothers, both working in the same nightclub, many years apart, both riding a bike in and back out? By god, we did. We thought that was pretty amazing and a great Roop something. It was almost as good as when he found out that I ran into a cute girl named Connie that worked at Carlo's Villa at Nottingham and Route 33. I liked Connie, and it turned out Ed knew her. Later on he fessed up to me that he dated her before I did when she worked at the White Castle at Arcadia and High years before. Well, we will leave it at that.

***

JERRY AND I HAD a blast travelling. Sometimes I would follow him and sometimes he would follow me. We always wanted to have our own car in case one of us wanted to stay wherever we ended up or if we joined another band. We continued to follow each other around Florida, and we agreed that Pizza Huts were the place to eat. There wasn't a great deal of them back then. There weren't nearly as many fast food places between Ohio and Florida, but there were always Pizza Huts.

Jerry, being a good Italian boy, dearly loved it. I've always liked just buttered noodles. We found out pretty early on at Pizza Huts we could get beer. He could get Italian stuff he liked, and I could always ask them if they would get me the wagon wheel noodles with garlic butter. Those were our meals all of the time. To this day I still like shells bowties or wagon wheels in garlic butter.

We would drive along, and Jerry would pull up beside me with the windows down and ask about a certain cassette tape. I would wing one over to him, and sometimes he would wing one back. We would somehow catch them or knock them down on our car seats. We travelled with little seven-once beers because they stayed cold. You could get one out of the cooler, and one was just right. Jerry would throw one of those little grenades in the window of my car and vice-versa. We couldn't do that today. We kept each other company and kept the boredom down to a minimum by sharing music, sharing beers and hitting those damn Pizza Huts.

***

IN MY FREE TIME I loved checking out Willie Pooch and Dave Workman,. They were just off the hook. Their band back then was called the Dave Workman Blues Band featuring Willie Pooch. They called me up. They didn't have a drummer for a night at Mr. Brown's on High Street on the south end of campus. That was the first time, other than maybe playing a song or two, I did the whole night with Workman and Pooch. I created a life-long friendship with both of them.

Willie and I spent, I suppose, thirty-five years together. I remember one day, oh, maybe ten years after that first night, at one of the Roop Brother parties, Willie told my dad, "Someday I'm going to take this boy out on the road. We're going to do a recording." Of course, later on, you will find that we did do that when we did our House of Blues tour. Willie never missed one of the Roop Brother parties. He was always there.

Workman has since gone out to California. He became friends with Carlos Santana and helps him out quite a bit as his guitar tech man, and plays in bands out there. To my surprise, Shelly who used to own Stash and Little Brothers when it was across the street from Dick's Den, was having a reunion with Workman. He was in town, and Barry Haden from the Dante's was in town, and she brought them up to Roop Brother's. I suppose this was six years ago or so. Shelly came up and wondered if I remembered her, I knew right away who it was; it was obviously Shelly. I gave her a hug and she said, "Well, we've got some friends here, do you know who that is? The guy in the nice black outfit with a nice black hat on?"

I said, "Oh, my god, it's Barry!" The Dantes were a great band. Everybody always thought they would give the Stones a run for their money if they didn't all get drafted like they did. And then Workman walks in and the band knew Willie was coming so they had another big reunion – Dave Friedlander and Rick Calura were playing that night. Workman had just got back from a couple weeks in Paris with Santana. He said life was good on the west coast, in that Workman fashion with his hair still looking like the zigzag man. What a talent! He said, "As long as I got enough money playing to drive my Alpha on Highway 1, life's good."

He said a cool thing about this Paris trip he had done with Santana. He knew that Carlos liked real good Cognac, and he bought him a bottle in Paris for a few hundred bucks. "I knew I was giving him something he liked. I didn't want anything in return. I just wanted to thank him for the trip and the gig, and how cool he is and being a part of his life. He says, 'Wait a minute.' And runs downstairs and comes back with probably an old Fender Telley, a nice, old Telecaster, worth a ton of money, even if it wasn't Santana's.

"Can you believe that for a gift? Workman smiled. "Shit, I just gave him a bottle, a good bottle, but it wasn't anything like a vintage Fender." Everybody sat in and played. It was quite the night.

***

THERE IS SOMETHING really cool about the seventies and eighties. Everyone's

friends, even my parents at times, would show up for your first night, even
if it was a Sunday or a Monday or a Tuesday, your first night of a month's stay
somewhere, everybody came out for your opening night. That was a big thing
amongst followers, friends and other musicians that would be off work or the
bartenders or the servers. Everybody stayed pretty tight and made opening
night special. They did that to honor us and make sure we had a packed house.

It was something we really looked forward to.

Probably around the same time of the Studio 5, Arlington, and Grandview
days, I liked the Scioto Inn. I played there with the Donnie Wilson band quite
often. The owners Sugar and Emory were a blast. Sometimes I would bartend
in the afternoons for them if they asked. I didn't have anything to do; I just
always left my drums there.

Oddly enough, one of the many acquaintances in Delaware, a buddy of
mine that I use to see drinking around town, Jim Gill, lived in a stone cottage
behind the Scioto Inn. This bar was across from the dam of Grigg's Reservoir.

There were four or five little stone cottages. Jim and his son, Ryan, have Chesron Chevy, GMC here in Delaware now. So, we were surprised to see each other up here from Columbus.

We had a hell of a good time between Studio 5 and the Scioto Inn, a crazy guy we knew did underwater construction, John Haselbaker. We left Studio 5 one day, and Haselbaker had a new Lincoln Mark IV. It was quite a car. The tires were all completely flat. He had once again pissed off a girlfriend. He must have left her at his condo to run out for a bottle or something. And she came up and let all of the air out of his tires. We were going over to the Scioto Inn, I think. He said, "That ain't going to stop shit. Hell, get in. She can't stop us." So we got in that nice new Lincoln and by god we did drive down there. And it didn't slow him down a bit. He had AAA come out and fix it.

One night I had my band booked at the Scioto Inn and I didn't want to pass up that job. But the band couldn't do it. I couldn't get anybody to fill in, so it was completely off for the Donnie Wilson Band. So I had the crazy idea to call Mom and Dad's buddy, the great sax man that I saw there in jazz trios, Chuz Alfred. I said, "Chuz, I got a booking at the Scioto Inn, do you think you can round up a guitar player and a bass player or something and we'll do this."

I was a little one hundred forty-pound skinny kid that drove him crazy on the patio when they hung out with Mom and Dad. But to my surprise, he called me back and he had the guys. And I just about shit. This was really something. A night of cooking jazz, no vocals. Just these great guys that just wanted straight swing, Latin, or shuffles. I loved the version of "Money Honey" he did.

Chuz was one of the most fun people to be around in the world. And if that wasn't cool enough, when the bar finally closed, Chuz is this witty, artistic, funny guy. We are standing out there by the van and saying good night; and he said, "Well, you got a van there. And you're in a band. And we're off work. Tell me that you have something for a night cap."

I did have something. I don't know what it was; it might have been a bottle of Boone's Farm Country Quencher. But we were drinking something and having a nightcap, and again, I thought this was too cool – partying with Mom and Dad's buddy, Chuz. Across the street was a long, narrow, cinder block building with real uniform small windows.

Chuz's imagination kicks in, he looks across at this long, low building with all of these matching windows and he said, "Well, if that damn train would

Me and Chuz

ever go by, I would get out of here." We were laughing and looking across the street, and it did look like a train at that time of night. I will say for a kid my age, getting to crank it up with him and then having some great laughs over a bottle or two of wine with him, and with that damn train car in the way, was pretty great.

Mike Flore is one of the best guys in the world. You have to see a picture of him, you can tell, he is one of the most mellow guys and one of best tenor sax players in the country, maybe one of the greatest tenor sax players ever. We had a lot of fun in Ohio in the late seventies before he moved down to the bay area, around St. Pete, Clearwater, Largo, Treasure Island, and Gulfport. Of course, he was the guy that I was with in the High Street Trio. We had played in many things together.

He was playing in Clearwater at a bar called Schlagers in a band called Mellow Madness. A guy named "Ard" Jerry Thompson was the drummer, and Danny Toller was the guitar player. The leader may have been Laddy, because

Mike always worked in Laddy's bands in Florida. He later was called Fat Laddy. If you get on the Internet for the bay area, the Tampa Bay, St. Pete bay area, and punch in Fat Laddy's bands, you will see what a life he had in the bay area. He hung out with guys like the Allman Brothers, Sea Level, and Roy Buchanan, and all of the guys who hung out up and down Highway 19. We had a ball.

Mike Flore

Mike was playing at this bar, and keep in mind the drummer, Ard, who would later be the drummer in Dickie Betts and Great Southern, and Danny would be the guitar player. Later, Danny Toller and his brother joined the Allman Brothers Band, as one of the drummers and second guitar player. I don't know when Warren Haynes came into the picture. Of course, these guys all hung out in the St. Pete area.

This band they had down there, Mellow Madness, was pretty kick-ass. During some of their songs you could let your mind wander off, like on the great one "Footprints." I don't really like to hear the original version, but these guys did a great version of " New York State of Mind." They did some great Herbie Hancock stuff, like "chameleon." Another one that seems weird but I liked was a great version of a song called "Disco Lady." Mellow Madness was a jazz, blues, funk, great, great Florida band. You don't see bands like that, except in the bay area.

The Sportsmen Bar on 19 I talked about, I can't think of what else it has been called, maybe Club 66, was a little free-standing building on the east side of the street, and you just never knew who you would run into there. Greg Allman, Dickie Betts, guys from the Bellamy Brothers, Sea Level, Roy Buchanan's band or guys from Laddy's band; you just never knew. Shlagger's was the bar where I met Jerry Thompson, Ard, the drummer that was in Dickie Betts; we had a great time.

One night we were sitting on the same seat, a half a cheek each, and playing his drums, or I would stand beside him and play high hat and snare, then we would switch back and forth. We had a great talk on break about how we were both playing actually correct, but it is interesting that some people like to be a little above the beat or a little below the beat; however, you interrupt where it is going, He could feel out which one of us wanted to push it or pull it back.

That was one hell of a band. This was at an absolutely beautiful nightclub, a downtown nightclub, dark, rich, fancy. Ard said, "Hey, man, I want you to have something to remember this night." And there was really nice print on the wall with a fabulous frame. He took it off the wall and said, "Here, remember this night." Then Mike Flore and I probably finished the night off sitting by the water somewhere having a beer. It was quite a time.

Greg Allman had given my buddy Mike Flore the nickname Craze. I could go in a bar and say, "Has anybody seen Greg or Craze?"

Another buddy that we had down there was Mickey, who had been on an album with Mike in a band called Melting Pot. As I heard the story in the seventies, he hit something when he dove into the bay, and that's how he ended up in a wheelchair. He went from a single-note player to one of the greatest slide players, because he could still do that. He was sitting in his wheelchair telling me once that he had gone up to Atlanta and was playing with Buchanan. Roy

liked the way he played slide. He had absolutely perfected it. In the middle of some greatness, he blows Buchanan's amp up. He slaps the arms on his wheelchair and said, "Isn't that just my fucking luck, you know, I'm kicking ass with Buchanan, and I blow his shit up."

Bartenders have different ideas for what is in a snakebite drink. In the seventies in South Florida a snakebite was what Mickey had on each side of his wheelchair, a bottle of schnapps and a bottle of Beam. He would pour a shot of one in your mouth, then a shot of the other one; you swish it around, and that was a snakebite. As we sat there, he would do a wheel stand off the stage with his wheelchair, and we were passing these bottles around doing snakebites with Mickey and having a ball.

It was not long after, in fact, we went down the road one day, me and a buddy, and found the house that was on the album cover of Dickie Betts and Great Southern. On the cover they were all sitting at a table by the fence in front of this plantation house. We got our picture taken drinking some whiskey

in the same corner where they were. My god, what a time! It wasn't too long after that they were playing in Columbus. A buddy of mine Sam Triplett and I were invited down to the hotel. I remember we walked on the floor they were on, and this big guy caught us, and we told him we were looking for Ard. He said "Well, I'll talk to Ard. He will be at the bar if he knows you." We went down to the bar and Ard came down, and we all got to go to the concert together. We were sitting backstage, and most of the road cases still said "Allman Brothers Band" on them. We were drinking wine and having a great time with the guys and reminiscing with Ard about our buddy Craze, Mike

Flore, in Florida. It was an incredible time.

I remember later on I was down there and Greg Allman pulled in, in a eighty-something Vette. It was dark green with chrome wheels. The license plate said, "Bay Bro." What a life those

Pier 66 Hotel

guys must have had!

Around 2009 Karyol and I were in Lauderdale and stayed at Pier 66 Hotel and Marina, I played there in the seventies and wanted see it again. The top floor cocktail lounge is now for parties only, but they showed it to me. It's very hard to believe that I was lucky enough to play there.

Not too long after that, the All-man Brothers got back together with Dickie. Danny Toller and his brother were also in the band. The new album was *Enlighten Rogues*. When they were at Leadgen Valley, I had the best seat of my life, sitting on a road case with Bonnie Bramlett beside Greg. He's amazing, his left foot just swinging around, while he enjoyed a hand full of nuts and a beer, still holding some chords, then a kickass solo, and back to the beer and nuts. Bonnie and I were handing a magnum of wine back and forth; Greg may have hit it also.

Me and Danny Toller

Being right there when he sang was something; he just took over, and it was definitely one of my musical highlights.

A friend of mine, Steve Mills, told me a story about Dicky Betts; this was in 2015. Steve's brother lives in Sarasota. One day at the Country Club he was at the bar talking with kind of a scruffy guy with his dog, all having a good time. Turns out it's Dicky. Dicky asked if he was going to golf, and would he like company? He said yes, and off the three go with a bottle. When they return to the clubhouse, Dicky disappeared for a few minutes and comes back with about a pound of bacon, and says that dog just loves bacon. Steve's brother said he is one hell of a good guy, fun to talk to, and a real good golfer.

***

I WAS JUST THINKING again of Mike Flore. One day we were out on Main out near Brice in Columbus, at Caesars playing. On the way home I had a bad idea. They hadn't quite gotten done building I-270 around the city yet. It was a little area from Taylor Station north of Broad to Hamilton, Taylor Station looped around and was running parallel with I-270, very close, and that's where the cement had stopped. South was dirt and from there north was finished cement but not open. We could see Hamilton Road about one-half, or three-quarters a mile away. We thought we could turn off Taylor Road right down through the construction dirt and get on the highway and just cruise on I-270 without going up the Hamilton Road. The cement was too thick, and we couldn't get up on it, so we drove between the roads thinking we could come up on the middle and pop onto I-270, and then just haul ass on the unopened I-270.

Well, we got stuck. We had to walk down I-270 to Hamilton Road. Back then there was a gas station that had a shop and a tow truck, thank god, a real gas station. We told him our problem and again, if it wasn't back then, we would have gone to jail, but this guy understood. He took us in his truck ,and we went down I-270 south in the northbound lane. It was closed, you know, unmarked and everything. What we were worried about was it is going to be daylight, and cops would see my bright red van sitting there in the median. But we got down there and got it hooked up and got it back down to Hamilton Road. We probably got home at six or seven in the morning and avoided being in some deep shit.

***

HERE'S ANOTHER ED MOMENT. After playing in Grandview one night, sometime after two in the morning, me, Ed and our buddy Jim Skillman, who had a company Neon Lights, decided to have some fun. We had a long night at the bar and we thought well maybe we will go up to the house and pick up this little piece of shit pontoon boat I had. It almost looked like it was homemade, probably only about twelve feet long with a seven horsepower motor, and it had plywood sides with very large Budweiser stickers on it. We hitched it up to my 1966 Corvette, also bright red. For some reason we thought it would be fun to put Budweiser down the side of it, the whole bowtie Budweiser logo, with white shoe polish, pulling this shit pontoon with

three of us. It was about daybreak by now, and we take it to the Scioto River by the O'Shaughnessy Dam and put it in.

My brother had this great idea of selling beers, shots, and hot dogs to people fishing all over the river. We are out there, and we got the grill going. I remember once I put a bunch of hot dogs on the grill, and we hit a little wave; and the grill dropped down into the charcoal, and Ed said, "There's no problem." He just wiped off the wieners leaning over the side of the boat, and put them back on the grill.

We cruised on, and it ended up with a sailboat race going on around us. We said, "Do you want beer or a hot dog?"

They yelled, "Maybe later."

We worked our way back into Twin Lakes just north of Shawnee Hill, which we really didn't know was an area you can't have a motorboat. There was a couple fishing, and we sold them a couple of double shots. I think those were only two bucks a piece, and beers were a buck. Ed had made a sign that said, "Mike Fink's Riverboat Franks - fifty cents." We sold them a couple of hot dogs, and I told them, "Don't tell on us, and we'll be here a lot of Sunday mornings, and we have beers and shots."

Then we heard the policeman up on the road, just north of Shawnee Hills at Twin Lakes. He called us up. Ed and me were standing there at the guardrail, letting us know about the no motorized vehicles. We looked down into the boat, and Skillman was laying down trying to hide the booze and stuff, but there is still a sign that said "Riverboat Franks fifty cents." Skillman came back up to the top. The policeman was disgusted and wrote us a ticket for the motorized vehicle, but to our surprise he didn't say anything about selling stuff there.

Jim said, "Well, you might remember me. I remember you; I was parking up by the power lines, just north from here in a yellow Chevy, with my girlfriend."

Then the policeman turned around and pointed the back of his ink pen to Jim, and said, "Now I remember, the b.j." And then he said, "Well, you got to get this boat out of here. I will meet you at the dock." It was right across the way, across from the girl's school.

So we headed over with a six or seven horsepower motor. It took us a long time to get over there in our piece of shit. He was mad as hell when we got there because it took us so long. I thought, what's he going to do when I start up a red Corvette with three guys riding in it, and Budweiser written down the side of it? But we backed it in, got the boat out of the water, and he gave us the ticket, and he said, "Don't even ever think of ever coming on this water again." Again, we were lucky.

***

AROUND THE SAME TIME, we loved playing at Flippo's Bar. Bob Marvin, who played Flippo Clown, had the Fireside at Reed and Henderson. One night Robin Redding was singing. She really didn't take any shit from anyone. She was beautiful with big brown eyes and straight palomino blonde hair, real long, and she was wearing a hot cream evening gown. Singers really didn't like people to take away from their music. The music was real important to all of us.

Most of the people who came to these bars came to see the bands, but once in awhile there would be somebody come in that didn't give a shit about what was going on onstage. That was okay if you sat in the back of the room; and you wanted to talk with buddies, but these guys made the terrible mistake of coming right up to a four top, right in front of the stage, right in front of Robin, singing her heart out for everybody and looking fabulous. I knew what she was thinking - you son-of-a-bitches!!! Why are you talking right in front of me when I am putting on my show? And I knew she was calling them every MF in her mind while she was singing, and knowing Robin I knew something was going to happen.

At the end of the set, the band was walking off the middle of the stage, right past these guys and they caught Robin' attention. She knew they never paid attention to her for the previous hour. They never looked up; they never applauded. But now that she was walking by them they decided to say, "You're just the best we ever heard." And I know she's thinking blow me! One guy said, "Oh, you just look like a fairy princess."

She cocked her arm like she had a magic wand in her hand and said, "That's right, poof, and you're a pile of shit." It was just absolutely perfect.

About the same time, I ended up being in a great band, a sixties and seventies cover band called Flashback. They were doing stuff like Tommy James and the Shondells, the Eagles, Chicago, Sly and Family Stone, Linda Ronstadt, Chuck Berry, Skynyrd, Blood, Sweat and Tears, Looking Glass, Zombies, Doors, C.C.R., K C and the Sunshine Band, Santana, and Hall and Oates. A hell of a lot of fun in that band. Fred Francis, Linda Epling, Daryl Gilk-

erson, and Steve Proman were a great band. I sure loved having my old buddy Daryl in the band; he was quite a character.

This is back when you joined a band, and they had about six shirts; you could still get them at Silverman's. You had to go down there and get the shirts, you had to have white slacks and black slacks, and you had to buy a Sure mic to match everybody else's, and show them that you were union.

We played Sangria North, Sangria East, and all of the Ramada Inns; they were some of the main stays. The Ramada South was a great place in Grove City on Springtown Road. As usual, the bandstand was behind the bar, and you could see everybody at the bar.

One night Scioto Downs had set a speed record. The place was just packed, everybody was drunker than shit, and having a great time. It was a big thing in the horse world that night. That lead me to a Roop idea. I stood up on top of my little drum seat, moved the ceiling tile over, acting like I was talking to the people in Room 205 above the band. The crowd was encouraging me on.

It looked like I'm talking to the people upstairs, so I decided to crawl up there, like I was going to crawl up into Room 205 with them. Hell, I was young; I hadn't had to repair anything yet. I didn't know what held dropped ceilings in, and the panels that sat in the middle of framework. I had the ceiling tile out of the way, and I pulled up on my elbows and that son of a bitch dropped over the band and over the bar, probably ten or twelve feet one direction, and eight feet the other direction. A bunch of the tiles fell on this bartender. I always knew she

didn't much care for me. I fell down on top of my drums and scattered them, and my cymbal went off the stage right past this bartender into the cooler. I noticed she was covered with the little white debris from the ceiling tiles, like powder all over her face, and I thought that was just funnier than hell. But the shit hit the fan. I just don't know how you describe it better than that, but the crowd had a great time.

That ended up costing me a little bit. I was probably making five hundred a week, which they took, and I think I still owed them another six or seven hundred. They put it on a tab for the coming weeks to play there. Well, that's the price you pay.

One day they left the linen closet open on the second floor, right across from my room. Bands didn't get the best rooms; we were near shit like the linen closet or the loud elevator. I thought, well, I've been playing for a couple of weeks for free because of my stupidity, breaking the damn ceiling.

 The linen closet was open. Like most vans back then, if you opened the back doors, underneath the bed that was built in, there was plenty of storage room.

I took the liberty of filling that with large towels, and a stack of folded sheets, towels, and pillowcases. A variety of stuff. It filled the whole back of my van.

A couple of weeks later I was driving down Sunbury Road, south of 161, where there is an "S" turn headed toward Morse Road. If you missed that turn you went way off into a ditch, way, way down into some people's front yard. A car had missed that and overturned. There were five or six people laying out in this yard on both sides of the driveway. Some other people were there, trying to help, and the emergency squad wasn't there yet.

Somebody said, "Do you have a towel, a blanket or anything in your car so we can help these poor people. They are bleeding." I opened up the backdoor of my van, and it looked like an emergency room storage cabinet. We put towels under their heads, and we had cloths and towels for other things. We covered them with sheets so they would stay warm, and I ended up leaving, but I always wondered what in the world the squads thought when they got there and these people scattered around this front yard were all covered in white linen from top to bottom, and their wounds were covered with fresh washcloths or towels. That worked out nicely. My investment for fixing the damn ceiling went to some poor people in trouble.

***

ANOTHER TIME WE WERE in Newark at a popular nightclub. The owner decided he didn't want to do the usual, with bands playing nine to two in the morning, doing forty minutes on and twenty minutes off. He thought he lost a lot of people on those twenty minutes off, so he thought he would split that in half and have the band take ten minutes off and not lose as many people.

So the band had a great idea, since he was so stupid, because we would just get started playing for twenty minutes and we would be taking a break. So the leader of the band started watching his watch. And at exactly twenty minutes, we would stop the song in the middle and take a break. We would come back ten minutes later and pick right back up with the last half of "Saturday In The Park." The owner realized we were making a mockery of him. And the shit hit the fan once again, but we went back to the normal sets after that.

***

SPEAKING OF MY BUDDY Daryl, you almost have to see a picture of Daryl to understand this chunky, longhaired, wonderful country boy, with a great laugh. He would always say, "I got a go home and bath the baby." One of my best friends. We weren't supposed to drink in the band, or we would get penalized. If you were late getting to the bar, you were penalized. If you were caught wearing your band shirt at a Waffle House or something at four in the morning, you got charged. Sometimes there were penalties just for fun, like if you messed up a lick in a song. The logic of not wearing the shirts was good because back then we probably had thirty bucks in each shirt, and the logic was to take it off when you are done playing so they all wore the same time, and not faded out.

One night Daryl and I were out behind a bar in Lancaster called The Orange Carpet. I had a VW bus with the door open in the back. Daryl and I had some rum and cokes. We were out there this one particular night, and we had our pink and white kind of quilted, cowboy shirts on with the pearl snaps and white Levis. These people were leaving, and once again Daryl killed me. He said, "Goddamn Roop, I think they thought we was a kissin'."There we were in stupid, pussy-looking pink and white quilted cowboy shirts. We would have been better off being allowed to drink in the damn bar.

Daryl and I had a code for four different four beat fills. When a brake was coming up, Daryl would show me two or three fingers, and that's the fill we would do. Drum and bass matched the fill.

We shared one room if we were in town. That's where we could dress or get our minds set for going down and kicking off the first set. So many times some guy would say, "Boy, that singer's hot." She would have her evening gown on and nice hair, which was a wig, eye makeup, they would say, "Oh boy, would I love to, you know, be with her." I thought oh my god, really? Poor gal loved to fish all day, then she would come in and change in our room. I'm thinking she still had the brown shit around her fingernails from reaching in the worm bucket,

and if you saw the clothes she kicked off and kicked over toward the tub just

Donnie Wilson Band at the Rickenbacker

prior to slipping into that evening gown, damn.

This goes back to the Donnie Wilson Band days. I loved to stop for a drink with Gene Deffenbaugh, the guitar player. We were quite good friends with Donnie and Vicki, but they would always go home after the job. We played at the NCA Club out at Reichenbacher Airport, the Copper Lounge, once a month when they would have a soul night, and we would get to open for whoever the band was.

On this particular night, it was a band called Sly, Slick and the Wicked that were currently opening for the O'Jays. They were using the O'Jays' equipment truck. So we all got to play on the O'Jay's equipment, and it was a fun night.

This band started so good I thought it was the Sly Slick and the Wicked, but three songs in here came these three tall, skinny brothers in these cool outfits, one yellow suit, one white suit, and one blue suit. They had square tuxedo tails, huge bell-bottoms, huge lapels and no shirts. That was Sly, Slick

and the Wicked. They came up and joined the band; and it was a lot like Earth, Wind and Fire, and we all hit it off pretty good. They asked if there was a cool place with a band we could all check out after midnight. We said we would meet at Joe's Hole on Main Street, not the greatest reputation there, but what the hell! We got there first from the air base, and the band was on a big stage behind a u-shaped bar.

They said, "Sly Slick and the Wicked from the O'Jays was in town tonight; and if we are real good, we might get them up here to play a couple of songs." There was still no sign of them, but, as usual, we had our matching shirts on, Gene and me. Gene leaned over and said that if they don't show up, we are dead. Sly Slick and Wicked showed up and played, and they invited us to play, and then we were okay. We got home safely it was a wonderful night.

***

ANOTHER NIGHT THAT WAS a blast downtown, again, me and Gene left the NCA Club and didn't have enough sense to go home or go play putt putt, which we did so much. We decided to go to the Needle's Eye. That was at Fourth and Main Street, behind Uncle Sam's Pawn Shop. It was a good little jazz bar. A townie bar downstairs with a jazz bar upstairs.

To my surprise, Gene didn't have any money, and I didn't have any money. I think Mr. Valentine was bartending. He had a cool grey fro that started halfway back, and I think his family had Gordy's and the Stardust too. We were shooting the shit with him; Gene was a good bull shitter. He said, "Well, is it possible we could cash a check, it's a government check. It's from the air base; where we just played; it was only for one night, so it wasn't much money, like two hundred eighty bucks or something," Gene said. "We are prepared, if we can cash this, to drink a bit. We are in the mood."

We got off from the NCO club, at probably eleven p.m. or something. So we had some time. I think he thought we were the craziest and the only white guys in the place, but there was a picture on the wall, a caricature of the Rusty Bryant, of the Night Train band, that my dad drew. It was signed "Nate Roop" with the date on it. I said, "If it makes any difference, my dad's name is Roop. He drew that caricature of Rusty."

He said, "Let me see your license." My license, of course, says Nathan Roop. He said, "Give me the check. Let's have some fun tonight," he thanked us, and he thanked my dad. Again, in this day and age, would that happen to two liquored-up idiots at Fourth and Main, behind Uncle Sam's Pawn Shop? God bless him. He cashes the check and we had, once again, a beautiful evening. We were playing at the Ramada in Perrysburg, Ohio, which was like a Las Vegas nightclub. It was absolutely gorgeous with great appetizers and a huge bar. Across the street was a Holiday Inn; it was also not your normal Holiday Inn bar. It had a lot of glass and marble, lots of custom neon lighting and stuff, like a Vegas show club. We were up there for a month.

Across the street at the Holiday Inn, they have somebody good, everybody kept saying, "When you have a day off, you ought to get over there."

What was cool was when two good bands like this were in town, one always had Sunday off and one always had Monday off, so there always was non-stop music in the neighborhood for the regulars. Sundays we could see them and visa versa.

Everybody said, "Man, go check them out." The weird thing was there were no cover charges back then, and these guys were getting a five-dollar cover. But they said, "Man, pay it. You got to see them on your day off."

So when our day off rolled around, probably the second week, we walked across the street, and we said, "Shit, this is a really good band." Then they introduced the singers, and they came out in sequined gowns, and a tuxedo, it was a hell of a show. They were a good band. I only saw them that once in the month we were there, but it was worth the five dollar cover and it was fun partying with people from our hotel over there.

It was probably five or six months later that I was at my folks' house, hanging out, in the family room watching some variety show on TV. Who knows what it was, but the usual seventies variety show. They were leading up to this, "Oh, this is a great band, If you haven't heard them yet, you will, please make them feel welcomed, the great Tony Orlando and Dawn." They came out and my jaw just hit the ground. Here it was the same damn band that was across the street from us in Perrysburg, and by God, they were on the TV. There was Tony Orlando and Dawn, maybe in the same sparkling evening gowns and tuxedo I saw them in. Pretty cool stuff, when you played that kind of shit because you loved your job, not what you played.

The Ramadas were always good to us, as I have said. And the Ramada on 161 in Columbus I was with the Post Raisin Band. It was my buddy Bob Mohney playing organ and this great singer named DJ. I think he was about four feet tall, maybe. I always thought he looked like Dudley Moore with his long hair, and he sang just like Barry White. It was just a great show band.

There were times when he had his tuxedo on and the guitar player and organ player would stand him up on top of the organ and pull his tuxedo drawers down to show his white boxers with red hearts. He would pull them up and jump down and sing some more, and he would run off the stage and come back with a chimp mask, gloves and feet on. He would walk out to the mic stand; everybody would get a kick out of him, and he would loosen the mic stand and start rubbing it up and down real fast. Of course, somebody in the band had to mention that if he kept that up, he would go blind. One of my favorites was when he would go backstage and come back between songs, dressed like a little soldier, and he would pull the trigger on a toy machine gun. The band made it sound like a machine gun as he would spin around in circles like he couldn't control the gun and fall down on the ground and roll off the stage. They just don't have stuff like that anymore.

***

THAT WAS ONE OF the hotels where we were near home, and we had foolish friends that helped us do dumb stuff. Bob, the organ player, had met a gal. We knew they were going to go to his room. I think it was me and the guitar player decided that we would get a twelve pack from the bar and go up and keep them company. Sure enough, they had all their pillows propped up and talking to us, but were not real happy. Me and another guy ran downstairs and got a love seat out of the lobby and took it upstairs, nobody caught us at 3:30 in the morning. We had to unscrew the legs to get it through the door, and put it at the end of the beds so we could all sit there with our beer, but it turned out Bob and his beautiful girlfriend had fallen asleep. We went down to the lobby and got six or seven foot trees in big planters, and put them around their bed. We knew they weren't going to have any sex, so we were happy and we left them. They woke up in the morning in a tropical jungle with a love seat in their room.

So later on we had a "get even" night. This time the guitar guy had met a gal and took her to his room. He had adjoining doors into the room me and Mohney were in, and we had 4ft DJ the singer with us. The guitar player came over, and we knew that his girlfriend was in bed for the night. She had her clothes off. We made up a story that that girl knew DJ, our little buddy, and that she was in the bed next-door naked and wanted him badly.

First, we told DJ that he should have a drink. We got him to have a couple of shots, and we did two or three shots with him, and we kept telling him, you know, she is expecting you to come over. We told him he should take all of his clothes off, and we got him completely naked.

We were ready to open the door and send him in. We said, "Are you ready?"

He was ready, and all revved up. He ran in and jumped up on the foot of the bed, and she looked out from the covers, and she screamed, and he screamed and they both screamed. He was standing there on the end of the bed stark naked, and his shit looked huge because his legs weren't very long. They scared the hell out of each other, and he came running back. That was just another one of those "get even" moments when playing in a band.

***

ANOTHER MID-SEVENTIES MEMORY that was a great one, especially since I am in Delaware now with my friends, was the first gig we ever had in Delaware with the Donnie Wilson band at a bar called Whitey's Nocturnal Bookstore on Spring, right across the street from the NAPA store and near the Ohio Wesleyan campus. A good friend of mine, Buffalo, ran it. Buffalo would end up being a friend for many, many years after that, at the Liberty Club. Me and Buffalo had a blast for years. In addition to the Donnie Wilson Band, we played there with the Willie Pooch Band. Sometimes where the railroad tracks went right by the Liberty Club, me and Buffalo and Pooch sat with a jug of wine, probably until the birds were chirping again.

***

THE DONNIE WILSON BAND, thanks to Buffalo, got some jobs on the OWU campus. I think it was the ATO House as they were the real hell raisers of Ohio Wesleyan University. They threw a great party. They were bringing out kitchen furniture to keep the bonfire going and just having a hell of a time. They had a trashcan in the bay window in the kitchen. The windows were open behind it.

It was a Harry Buffalo party. We would walk by the can and dip our plastic cups down in and fill it up. As the night went on, some other house in the neighborhood had decorated the Harry Buffalo with a dead rat. A girl and her boyfriend went to dip a cup in and get a drink, and pulled up the rat. They screamed and threw their cups, and she threw up all over the place. But being the good drinker that Gene Defenbaugh our guitar player was, he just stuck his cup back down in, and pulled it up, took a big drink and said,

"I don't see what the problem is; that is a healthy rat." He just chugged his, and I think then more people puked. Oh, some fun in Delaware.

***

ANOTHER STRANGE NOTE, the Donnie Wilson Band loved playing at J. Charles' Scotch and Soda on Hamilton Road around the back of the shopping center, just north of the airport a little bit. You drove around the back, and there was this bar. This was a special night because it was St. Patrick's Day, and he had put ads in the newspaper and everything. I had been in Florida with a friend of mine. I thought it would be fun to let J. Charles know where I was, even though I knew I was going to get back in time to play. I asked the operator when I called to reverse the charges to J. Charles' Scotch and Soda, and had asked for him. I had told her the situation. She said, "I have a collect call for you from Al Roop in Fort Lauderdale, Florida."

And he said, "Oh, oh," I could hear him say, "That's bad."

I said, it's okay, just have a car at the airport a little after eight p.m. to pick us up. He was freaking out about all the green beer and everything. But he was over there and picked us up and he said, "You stupid son-of-a-bitch. You are just trying to get my goat!" When we got back to the bar, he thought I was pulling his leg, and that it was a set-up. He said, "Weren't you in Florida?"

I had filled both of my front pockets of my Levis up with sand and shells from Florida, so I emptied both of my pockets on his floor. I also had the pamphlet from the back of the seat from the airplane of how to buckle your seatbelt, crash positions and all of that. Then I guess he believed it, and that led to shots and fun with the Donnie Wilson Band and our buddy J. Charles. The Scotch and Soda is still there to this day, and it is probably the best bar in Gahanna. I've been going there since the mid-seventies.

***

WE HAD A BUDDY, YOGI Cowan. Yogi was a great sax player, a great organ player and a great singer. He could do anything. He could play funk, jazz, anything. He was at the Ohio Theatre for a Blood, Sweat and Tears concert, you can't make up shit like this. He is digging on the band, sitting in the front row of the balcony and all of a sudden, Yogi's doing the alto-sax solo from the balcony along with Blood, Sweat and Tears. He really could have been in the band; he was just that good. But of course, they didn't think Yogi should be there any longer, and he had to go.

That's a long line of crazy Yogi shit. He was playing at the Oakland Lounge once, a little beer joint, playing a Hammond B-3.

Somebody said, "Where in the hell is Yogi?"

They said, "Well, he is way up in that oak tree out in front. And I think he's got a pint of whiskey." Sure enough Yogi was up in the oak tree, drinking his whiskey having a great time. They got him down and he played, after a few pushups.

There was a bar on Fourth, right across the street from the Sugar Shack, called Positively Fourth Street. They had the cream of the crop guys in there, kick-ass bands playing, and there goes Yogi. He walks up, gets on the stage. You could see him talking to the keyboard player and the keyboard player shaking his head, "No." Yogi's got his hand in between his hands, playing probably what was absolutely perfect to be played, but the keyboard player still doesn't want to let Yogi sit in. So Yogi backs up for a minute and then walks back across the stage and picks up the guy's soprano sax at the right time to butt in. He starts wailing and again; he should have been in the band; but he picked the wrong time to think he could pull that off, once again out he goes.

I went into the Harley House Hotel at 161 and I-71. Boy, they had some bands. Yogi said, "Hey man, you've got to check out my van. Every night I go out and put another gallon or two of Bondo on my van, I just trowel it out with this big trowel, getting rid of the bodylines on the van. You can't tell whether it's a Ford, a Dodge, or a Chevy anymore." He was so proud of it. It must have had twenty gallons of Bondo on it, that's what he did with his crazy energy at night. He was just putting more body putty on this damn van so you couldn't tell what it was. Oh, that's old Yogi Cowan.

***

THIS GOES BACK TO, 1978, I imagine, something like that. We had played in Denver again, why I don't know, because I didn't much care for my early experience there. But I had a really cool van. I loved to build neat interiors in vans that I had. A buddy of mine, Rob Dixon, the greatest painter I ever met, a

McGuffey Lane on my bus 1978

great airbrush painter, had a shop in Powell, the Mirage Garage. I built the

interior in this van with ivory carpet, gold mirrors, dark oak trim and a bar in the back, and that's what I was travelling in. Dixon painted a mural around the van. It was a short Chevy, no windows at all and candy red. He did scenes of Las Vegas around it from brochures. He had every logo and classic symbol of Las Vegas all the way around it from the "Welcome to Vegas" sign, the Stardust, the Golden Nugget, Caesars, the Riviera. On the back doors it had a showgirl that just looked gorgeous, by the license plate, it had a perfect bottle of Jim Beam, You could even see the date on the bottle. It was a beautiful van. Some friends of mine said, "You ought to drive it to Vegas."

***

IT WAS QUITE A WAYS to Vegas, but I did drive it there and drove around town a bit. People loved the van. I was drinking with a guy down around Circus Circus, and there was a little bar in front of it that was known for their one-pound hot dogs for a buck. He delivered tickets for free breakfasts and shit all over town; that was a big deal. He said, "Boy, you ought to go see Binion at the Horseshoe, maybe he would be interested in it for people delivering his complimentary tickets around town."

I pulled into the Horseshoe's valet parking and was told, "Just leave that van sitting right there." It looked cool in front of the big places. I went in, and I had pictures of the van with pictures of the Horseshoe on it. It was beautiful. I asked if I could see Mr. Binion.

They said, "Wait just a minute." They were probably checking security, all kinds of stuff out. They came back; I had gotten their attention because I mentioned that I had something that he would be interested in. They said, "Mr. Binion is in the dining room right now, if you go across the hallway to that phone, we will patch you through to him."

I told them, "I have some pictures he would be interested in." I didn't realize in the seventies that was probably the dumbest thing some stupid kid from Ohio could do in Las Vegas is challenge Mr. Binion with, "I've got some pictures you might like to see."

Immediately there was a couple guys there to whisk me off to a room where I saw surveillance things and a catwalk going to this office and they said, "Who is this guy that sent you; what does he look like? Short?" I said he was kind of a middle-aged guy.

They said, "How middle-aged? Why did he tell you to come here?" Boy, they put me through the ringer. They didn't want to know anything about my van. They wanted to see the pictures, and once they saw the pictures all they wanted to know was what this guy looked like that told me that I should see Mr. Binion about a van. Then I realized I might be scared shitless. But as it worked out, they realized I was no risk to them; they were very nice. I had no idea who the stupid shit was who told me to go there. I got to see the back scenes there a little bit, which was an eye-opening adventure.

I did sell the van to Valley Van Works in Las Vegas; he gave me some cash and wrote me a check for the van, and I got a ticket to get the hell back home. I was glad that nobody took my ass out for being a dumbass, saying I had pictures they would like to see.

***

HERE'S ONE OF MY favorite Ed moments. Ed and I both loved racing. We loved the Ford 500 when it was in downtown Columbus with the road race-cars and Indy cars running the streets. We watched them from the old Ohio Penn; we found a small brick building that housed the electric chair (Old Sparky) and the last night cell.

We loved the Mid-Ohio track too. I was with some friends and apparently my brother had been ahead of us with some friends, waiting to get in for the Indy cars. We were waiting on that little two-lane road that comes into the track, and you just wait and wait and wait at like six or seven in the morning. We saw this guy by the side of the road. How fucked-up do you have to be to be laying on the side of the ditch with a goofy blanket wrapped around you? He was just sawing logs. It was like an Indian blanket, and everybody was just driving by him. Several hours later I'm walking through the pits, and here comes my brother with a big buzz on, and he's got this goofy Indian blanket wrapped around him. It was still a little chilly in the morning. He says, "Hey, Al, what do you think of my serape?"

I said, "Holy shit, you were the guy that was laying out in the ditch asleep when we came in."

He said, "Yea, they kicked me out of the car. We bought a couple cases of White Castles to come up here, and I was killing them so they kicked me out of the car. The car went on forward and I never knew where it was. I just slept there by the ditch and eventually came in." There was my brother, just having a ball.

*****

PLAYING IN AND OUT of town were great days. We got rooms, we got half-off on food and you got to know the bartenders - boy, we got some deals on drinks. We didn't have to move our equipment for two weeks to a month. Sometimes, when you were there for two weeks, we got a two-week extension and the next place would just pushed it off a couple of weeks. It was really a great life. We could make our rooms the way we wanted, move in. Hotels didn't have anything but beds and a bathroom back then. I kept a little fridge in my van that I would take in and oh maybe a lava lamp, a record player, and you had to have an iron to take care of your clothes.

We each had our own cool little apartment. We would bounce back and forth. The first thing that you had to do was try to find a laundromat near a bar that had burgers. You would get a greasy burger, a beer and do your stage clothes and stuff. We could rehearse a couple of days a week in our rooms.

I usually didn't room with anybody; but this one month in Dayton I did. We thought let's put those huge bed spreads up over the windows, and we completely blacked the room out. We watched TV, listened to good music because we brought our stereo in the room, and we could order a late break-fast or burgers; we could even have a case of beer. It was a challenge between us. By the time we went to the bar to play at nine p.m., it was dark again. We just hung out in the room for a week, going one week of our lives with never seeing daylight, just food, beers, good TV and music, and then go do the gig.

In Indiana we worked at the Sheraton airport. It was pretty cool because we could sit in the top floor bar in the afternoon; and after the traffic drive reporter was done, he would buzz the top floor with his helicopter, land it, then he would come over for a drink. We were there about a month and knew everyone that worked there. For fun we would go to the end of the runway a couple of times of week, take a grill out there, cook burgers and watch the planes come in.

I always enjoyed watching planes come in. I've gone out to Port Columbus many times. It's especially fun at Port Columbus to watch the President's plane come in. That's a bad-ass airplane. Sometimes a couple of the bartenders came out with us. We were cooking out by the runway, and they brought brownies. We had burgers, beer and some kick-ass brownies, I'll say.

By the time I opened the bar, it was good that I had many years to watch restaurant bar managers and food and beverage managers from the stage. So many of them were jackasses to the band and to their own staff. You could watch them screw with waitresses and bartenders. Sometimes they would stand in the back of the room, and if they thought we were too loud for the people eating dinner, they would put their hands over their ears and point at us, "You're too loud."

But I'll tell you when you play songs like Chicago's "Color My World" a thousand times a year, you tend to play by second nature; and it just goes on, and you get to daydream watching the room and the managers.

Occasionally, I'd watch the people who started out, maybe a table with two couples; they were having fun, then they become not so much fun for each other or for us.

Or the businessmen who come up and take the front table and become butts. Between nine p.m. and two a.m. you could see a huge transformation of the bar manager and some patrons. But that probably helped me by the time I got my own bar, I kind of knew how not to be one of those dicks, I hope.

My sister, Ginny, mentioned several times, often tells people that she made me the good drummer that I was. She extended my arms quite a bit. She said she made it possible for me to have that long reach because she lifted me up by my arms so much it made them long, God bless her. Get her and my nieces together, Shelly, Natalie, and Melanie, and Ed nicknamed them the "June Taylor Dancers" after the Jackie Gleason TV show because nobody could beat these four gals dancing. In a bar that we were playing in or at one of the Roop Brother

Nieces - Mel, Shel & Nat at the Slippery Noodle on the Pooch Tour

backyard bashes, the June Taylor Dancers were always having a ball.

***

WE WERE TALKING ABOUT the bars in Florida and how things in the early days were so much different. Some of the great cocktail lounges we worked in Fort Lauderdale included the Pier 66 Hotel by the yacht club. Back then we played at places like that. It was amazing. If you came in and you looked nice; but you only had a polo shirt and slacks on, you couldn't get in. But they had a rack of sport jackets that were left there. You could always slip into a sports jacket and come on in and have a good time. Some of the other places like that if you came in with a t-shirt you couldn't get in, but there was a rack of collared shirts, in any size, and you could put a collared shirt over your t-shirt and go on in. Boy, you couldn't do that anymore. I'm sure the health department would not like you reusing shirts.

***

I LOVED BUSES, tour buses. Me and a buddy of mine built a tour bus that we used quite a bit. There was a lot of misuse of the bus, like taking it to the Silver

Dollar Saloon on 161 and using it as a car. When we were leaving my buddy Sammy Triplett thought that he could drive it, even though it was a thirty-five foot long and had a four-speed stick shift. I happened to look in the mirror and I noticed that he caught a car with the rear bumper and pulled that car to a car that pulled that to a car, and we got him stopped. Nothing was hurt. It was a beautiful bus that had been an ex-Greyhound; it only seated twelve people with a full beautiful bathroom, a back den, cabinets in the middle, an L-shape with a bar, TV, microwave and fridge. It had all the goodies and really nice seating in the front area.

Once when nobody was using it, our friend Paul Yoakum was coming back from a NAPA paint conference or something. He needed picked-up at the airport so Dave Thatcher, Marsha Jones, John O'Brien, and a bunch of us went out to the airport, again something that would never happen these days. But back then it was a very different world. So we pull in and park right in front of the airport, and nobody gave a shit. It turns out this is about the time that Robert Redford was filming a prison movie called Brubaker in a nearby deserted prison. Somebody told us that we had to move the bus and somebody from the bus said we were waiting for Robert Redford, and we were good to go. Here Yoakum comes out, he wonders why there was such a nice fanfare greeting for him coming out to the bus. We got out of there and continued on.

It might have been about the same night we had the bus sitting in downtown Delaware, and we thought it would be fun to shoot the alley beside O'Brien Olds, and see if we could get out the backside over toward Franklin Street. We were able to do that, then we thought we would back it into the alley beside the Jug to the east, and go to the Jug. We got it stuck sideways between the Jug and JoAnn's Barbershop. We got scared so we jogged it out on the road and ran down to the Campbell House Hotel like we were hiding a 35-foot bus. We parked it out back and went in.

Another great time had something to do with Bill Yoakum, who hired the bus to go to the World Series of Rock in Cleveland. Since it was a bus, we got really cool parking right downtown. And one of Yoke's buddies, John, I believe, said he would rather hang out with me. So we climbed up the hinges of the door to get on the roof and leaned against the air conditioners, drank beer and listened to the concert. Underneath us was a hot buttered beef stand. We would drop money down to them, and they would wrap up in foil these great hot buttered beef sandwiches, and throw them up to the roof, ah hell, we were riding high on the hog. We could hear the concert, eating well, and it felt good leaning against the air conditioners.

One thing that didn't go too good for the bus is when McGuffey Lane, our very good friends, were thinking about buying it. It's was probably about 1980 or 1981, and they started using the bus. They got a driver and said the guy was good. He was a truck driver, and they had insurance on it. They went to Tennessee to play, and on Thanksgiving Day I got a phone call that there had been an accident and the bus had hit a hotel, the Bilmar in Nashville. I would have to go get it. The band found other transportation home, and the hotel wanted the owner to come down and get it. The band was sponsored by a production company that was paying for everything so me and my best buddy Dave St. Clair on Thanksgiving went to get it.

We put a bottle of wine and a bottle of Schnapps in my briefcase; we took some chains and a little winch thing, and got on the bus to go to Tennessee. The bus was full, and we got separated; but one thing good happen when they said, "Well, we are loading another bus next door for the trip."

Dave and I dove off that bus, got our shit and got on the other bus, and it turned out that there was only eight or ten people on it. Everybody soon was comparing what they had. Somebody had a bottle of Jack Daniels, and I said, "Well, we got some wine and some Schnapps."

I remember this gal was driving the bus, she yelled back, "I smell that back there." I went up to talk to her, leaned on the dashboard and told her we had an old Greyhound 4107 that we were going to get, and that it hit a hotel in Nashville. She was a good driver, and we enjoyed the ride. She didn't really give a shit what we did.

We got down there, and it turns out that they had backed the bus in this U-shaped hotel with the lobby in front. They started the bus up the next day, and they didn't have any air pressure and the wheels weren't chalked, so it started going toward the lobby. They panicked and rode it into the lobby. Luckily, they hit about the middle of the windshield and a corner of the building or it would have just gone right through the damn building. The night shift hotel guy said he was taking a nap and said, "Damndest noise, it about knocked me off my little cot!"

The driver's window and both the windshields were gone, it was about fourteen thousand dollars of damage. The only window that wasn't broken was in the door to get in. But when we were leaving the parking lot, I didn't have that cam locked shutting the door. I pulled out swinging left and the damn door flew open and hit a sign. Wouldn't you know, the only window that wasn't broken on the front of bus.

So we drove it home on a Sunday. We took back roads through Kentucky driving the bus with sunglasses, front mangled and the windshield, the headlights, everything broken. We drove on in the next morning, and we went to the production agency in Grandview; and they said, "We didn't remember that window on the door being broken."

I said, "Oh, yea, this is how we found it." That was that window that I screwed up by not having the damn door locked.

But anyhow, McGuffey Lane took care of it; and John Schwab occasionally at their reunions still mentions, "We've done a lot of shit. We've even wrecked a bus." And it always makes me feel proud.

One day we took the bus to Legend Valley; it was Molly Hatchett and a bunch of other bands. It was so rainy when we pulled in. They took a big bulldozer and pushed us up there by everybody else's bus. I remember, we were sitting in there having a drink. Some guy from Molly Hatchett came running into the door of our bus, and it was sitting kind of low because it sunk in the mud. He bottomed out on the staircase and went face first under the driver's seat. Somebody picked him up and said, "Hey, wrong bus, Dude."

And he just fell back out the door. We never saw him again.

Probably my favorite time out there was for Cheap Trick and Todd Rundgren. I was loaning the bus to A&M records, and my brother and St. Clair were with me. We hit it off with the guys. My brother, and Dave hit it off with Rick Nielsen, which makes sense, all funny guys. Carlos Bonn invited me on his bus and, my god, that was a beautiful bus. It had everything, valences over the windows, everything was all inlaid in mother of pearl, like a guitar. Holy shit, were we comfortable.

One of the most disappointing things ever at Legend Valley was when my friend from Florida Danny Toller was playing guitar with the Allman Brothers. And at that point, it was Dickie Betts and Danny Tollar playing together.

StClair, Nelson, Ed Roop

I had a Mirage Garage jacket on, that was the custom shop that painted my vans. He had a brown satin jacket with gold letters embroidered "Allman Brothers Band." We traded jackets, and I was so happy to have that jacket, but I looked for it in the bus the next day, and it was nowhere to be found. That still sucks that I don't have that jacket.

***

WE WOULD OFFER TO take fans from the Bogey Inn to Reds games in the bus, ten people at a time. On the way over I made the sandwiches up and stuck them in the frig, and stocked it with beer. St. Clair was driving, and one time before he got to the stadium he thought the motor was blowing up. What it was was a fan blade came off and made the motor run so rough, he had to drive on the berm. He couldn't go very fast because it ran so rough.

It was all out of balance. He got it to the stadium and my buddy from Ernie's North/South Truck Stop here in Delaware picked me up at Powell Road and 23. I was living on Powell Road at the time. He had this monster, semi-hauling tow-truck. We flew probably ninety miles an hour to Cincinnati. We backed up to the bus; he pulled the rear axles out so he could tow it. The group came out of the game, and they got on the bus. I could lean over and look in Bobby's mirror. I could see St. Clair sitting in the driver's seat of the bus just with his arms folded cruising along, hitting his beer. The front wheels were off the ground behind us, a thirty-five foot tow truck pulling a thirty-five foot tour bus. We are dragging these people back to German Village; this guy was a good enough driver. He pulled down this side street in German Village to where they wanted to be dropped off, and we were on time, then we drove it home. My hat's off to that great driver.

My buddy John O'Brien, of O'Brien Oldsmobile in Delaware, had some friends in New Jersey. He thought that one of them wanted to buy the bus. They were having a seafood party, and we were invited over to take a promo package for the bus. We were pretty excited to get over there. We get out to the airport, and we run into our buddy John Green, John Wayne Green, from Delaware. He was the bartender at the old Port Columbus Airport bar, when it was a cocktail lounge on the far right. We had some drinks with him; then we headed for our airplane and sure enough, dicking around with John, we missed the plane. We got back to John, and he was laughing his ass off. We were using pay phones and the bar phone, no cell phone yet, trying to get flights; we are trying everything.

All we could come up with was a train that left Crestline around eleven at night for the east coast. We were ready to get there. Yoakum and his girlfriend said they would come and get us. So we get in the car with them at some point in time and headed for Crestline, Ohio, up near Mansfield. There was no train station there, but this train was supposed to come into this stop. We see a train light coming so we go and stand on the other side of the cement where you can tell you were supposed to go, we thanked and said goodbye to Yoakum, and this son of a bitch freight train just hauls ass by.

There was a YMCA right there that had a diner. Yoakum had left; he thought that was our train. So we walked over to the YMCA and they said, "That train was running a little early. It went through earlier. So you have no train."

There were some local boys shooting pool. The Y was the only thing near the rail yard. Luckily, O'Brien had a bottle of wine in his briefcase so we had wine to drink, and shooting pool at the YMCA until Yoakum got home so we could call him again, again no cell phones. He comes back to take us to Port Columbus, where we had a morning flight out of town. We get back to Port Columbus, and twenty hours later we finally got to New Jersey. Of course, the guys aren't waiting for us at the airport anymore. They had to come and get us. We missed the seafood fest, and it turns out they weren't interested in the bus. Later John Green was the bar manager of the Playboy Club in Columbus in the old Desert Inn by the Kahiki.

***

ABOUT 1980 I PLAYED at the Brown Derby Restaurant in the Lounge on Morse Road. It was a great place. I played there with Yogi Cowan. I didn't know Vasili yet but it was his place at the time. Thirty-four years later I would meet my very good friend, Vasili Konstantindis at Buns Restaurant in Delaware. He had the Brown Derby for quite some time. We shared stories at Buns about some of the employees he had there.

We had to have crossed paths because we had the same Greek buddies, Captain Nicki of Fisherman's Wharf, and Nick Tornick of Nick & DPs and the Whisky Still on 161, a fun bar to work at. Nick's son George was a good friend; he later had the VIP. So over thirty years later at Bun's I told Vasili a funny story about his buddy Nick.

I said, "Boy, Nick got me in some trouble there with a bartender. I thought she was kind of cute." I think Nick was laughing his ass off knowing the outcome would be bad. I remember it was a Valentine's Day because she had already broken my key off in the door of my car so I wouldn't leave the bar in the afternoon. She called a locksmith in and had my key replaced with a red key so I would remember her, and that it was Valentine's Day. One thing led to another, and when I got off work, we went to her place. Later I wanted to go home. I had a big day and night. I got up and I couldn't find my Levis or anything.

She said, "They are in the freezer. I will thaw them out and wash them in the morning and cook you breakfast."

And I said, "Oh, I've got to go."

She said, "Well, that's probably not going to work." I went downstairs and sure enough, pants, shirt, socks, everything had been run under water and were in the freezer, so I gave in and stayed. I took my new red car key, my freshly washed clothes and finally got the hell out of there. That just makes Vasili laugh his ass off. So, I'm glad to share that story for him; he had said it must be in the book. I'm sure I got even with Nick.

Another buddy of Vasili and mine was Captain Nicky at Fisherman's Wharf. Bob Mohney and I played there as a duo, and Captain Nicky would come up on stage. I will never forget the day he said, "I'd like to sing the song 'Please Release Me, Let Me Go.'" The timing on it is the regular 4/4, but he sang it in some 3/4 or some crazy shit. Mohney just looked over, shrugged his shoulders and said, "It's Greek to me; I don't know." But we had a blast with Captain Nicky and old Nick. God bless him.

***

IT WAS LIKE 1983, and I was getting good jobs from booking agents and promoters, and the promoter that did the Ohio State Fair had me help with the Beach Boys. My all time idol was Dennis Wilson, the drummer, who had passed away diving in the bay beside his sailboat in 1983. I got a chance to go and pick up the Beach Boys. It was quite a highlight of my life. I took a large window van, and I was supposed to go out to Executive Jet Aviation on the back of the airport. Come into the Hamilton Road gate and Executive Jet was right there, I pulled up to the fence by the tarmac and went inside and the attendant said he didn't know of any plane coming in. He had nothing on record coming in. He asked me if I had the tail number of the plane, I didn't. I just

Beach Boys Plane

knew that I was supposed to be there about eleven p.m. He said well, "Just hang out; and if I hear anything, I will let you know." He was sitting in a dark room looking at this board all lit up with planes coming and going. It was pretty neat to see the operation. Here he comes out and says, "I've got your plane. They are on approach. They are about five miles out."

They had left the east coast, the Jersey area or something, without a flight plan because if they would have turned in a flight plan, there would have been a penalty for leaving an airport in their big Martin 44 turboprop, because of noise restrictions that late at night. I guess, not to have a flight plan was better, just get the hell out of there and take their chances later. He said, "Sure enough your plane is coming in." The attendant opened the gate for me so I could pull the van in, and here comes this big passenger plane. It probably would seat a hundred or so. It had a stairway that dropped down out of the tail of it so they didn't need assistance. Here comes Mike Love holding his clothes over his shoulder and Carl Wilson and all the guys coming down the steps with their friends. I suppose they had about twenty friends. They got in the van, and we took them to the hotel. They did an afternoon show and a later show, and then I took them to the hotel.

The next day the promoter threw a party for them. He had an ice carving of a woody, and surfboards. It was at the Marriott North up by the Budweiser Plant just north of Columbus. My brother looked a hell of a lot like Mike Love. They were both younger then, and they both had the same blonde hair. We were teasing them about looking alike, and seeing my brother and Mike side by side was something.

I worked many things with the Beach Boys for a few years. One of the fun nights I had was

Mike Love

getting the hotel ready for the band. There was a code word for how you got in touch with their manager at the hotel desk. I would take the room roster and put colored dots by the band's names, nothing went by names, it went by colors, and their luggage had the same color tag on them. The blue would go to the blue room, red-to-red and yellow and so on. The guy that was showing

me this said, "You might as well go to the lounge and hang, and wait because it never works out the first time." I told the bartender I might get a call from the desk.

He said, "Well, you're right. You've

got a phone call." Red won't be on the same floor as blue; green was supposed to be down by the workout center because bands like that, because after hours they could have the workout center or pool to themselves. Sometimes we would have to work out stuff like leave the plane sitting at the airport and charter a bus to go to a nearby city. They had two sets of equipment, truck A and truck B. One set of equipment might be at the fairgrounds and maybe the other in Dayton, and all set up. Then back to the hotel in Columbus, then take hotel vans to the plane the next day. The A and B trucks would stay ahead of each other for the next jobs.

Mike Kawalski

I had became friends with Mike Miros and Mike Kawalski at the Ohio Theater. I'm proud and tickled I still get a Christmas card from Mike and Dawn Kawalski; he was a drummer for many years, off and on. The Beach Boys were playing at the Ohio Theatre so they must have been staying at the Hyatt right beside it. They came down from their rooms, and I was going to walk down the hallway that connected the Hyatt to the Theatre. Mike Love said, "Oh, no, ride with us in the limo." So I rode with them down the alley, a half a block. We went into the Ohio Theatre, and there was a beautiful room full of roast duck and mangos, cheese, carrots, salads; an incredible array of food, liquor and iced-down beers. They said you might as well help yourself. Usually, we weren't allowed to touch any of that. It's something the band demands to be there for friends or whatever, but they don't partake in any drinking, and they don't let the other guys in the band do that either. Boy, I was in heaven.

Carl & Gina Wilson

I checked it all out and had a good time.

One of the coolest things ever was Mike called me over and said sit down and try out my new drums, and I did. Another time the group was back, I really liked Carl Wilson. His wife was Dean Martin's daughter, and they wanted to eat somewhere nice. Of course, I took them to Captain Nicky at Fisherman's Wharf. Captain Nicki and his staff took great care of them. He could take a bottle of champagne, not quite open it, set it on the table; and he could count down when that cork would go.

Another time we were there with Bruce Johnston and a couple of the other guys. The Anchor Inn across the street had the Rusty Bryant Band with Hank Marr. Hank Marr was one of the great Hammond B-3 organ players. Mike Kawalski was going to lay over in town the next night; he wondered if there was any chance, while we are in town, that I could get them to

play on their night off so he could sit in with Marr. I talked to the guy who owned the Anchor Inn, and band said yes they would play at seven the next night. They weren't supposed to tell anybody we were coming but they did; and we pulled in, and the place was packed.

Everybody was there thinking the Beach Boys were going to show up, but it was Bruce, Mike and myself. Mike got to play a set with an idol Hank Marr. I told the Anchor Inn people that they kind of screwed over Mike; he bought the band for a quiet night. Hell, they usually only had forty people in there, and here they had a hundred fifty people in there. When Mike was done, we asked, "Is this the way to the kitchen?"

And they said, "The kitchen is not open."

I said, "We don't want the food; we just want to get the hell out." My car was parked back there, and I remember we got in the car and Bruce said, "God bless you Al for tinted windows." And we got the hell out of there and again we went across the street to Fisherman's Wharf.

***

ANOTHER HELL OF A PLACE to play has always been Buckeye Lake, even before people knew the new bars, like Pappa Boos and Captain Woody's. When Ed and I started going there, the ballrooms were still there. They had a crystal ballroom and the pier ballroom. Louie Armstrong and other great people played there.

There was a little beer joint that folks would go in called the Pink Elephant, but that ended in the early sixties. The big one called Pappa Boos on the north shore was a great little place, part of it still stands. The main old house was called Club 51. In the seventies and eighties, and next door to it, Captain Woody's, was called Walt's Landing. Bob and Judy owned Walt's Landing. They would go up to Lake Erie to fish, and they would bring the fish back. They just had a pool table out on the front porch. The Blue Goose was still there, the legendary place for turtle soup; we had a ball playing there in the Barrel House Band.

Hunt's Landing is gone now, that was right around Cranberry Marsh, and

Smitty's on Seller's Point was a tremendous place. The Copper Penny which is still there on the south shore; and down a canal on the far south eastside was the Port Bar. Now it is the Port Bar BBQ; the gang there is just the best. I have gone there before, and they would say, "Well, we are closing. Do you want a case of beer? We will leave the stereo on, throw some more logs on the fire, and we will cook you breakfast in the morning, but we are getting the hell out of here." That's a memory of the Port Bar that I have with Mark, Mike, Sue, and their dad.

Ed always had a boat by the Blue Goose and eventually me and Ed and Skillman had a pontoon together out there for probably fifteen years. And if we had too much to drink, we could always pull into the Port Bar and sleep on the boat and just have the time of our lives around a bon fire. One night with my brother after the Port closed, around the fire, we met Red from Columbus. A good ol' long red haired guy that had one of only small old campers there; I drank with him before. I said, "Red this is my brother Ed."

He said, "Hi Ed, I'm Red, that's my shed, that's my sled, where are we gonna get some head, Ed." He's listening to David Allen Coe around the fire.

In fact, once just a couple of years ago, we rented a pontoon boat from the old Sailor's Marina, Boat Boy's. Me and my buddies, our geezer group, Gary Gray, Dave Thatcher, and Rick Long. We were cruising down this canal that goes back behind Harbor Hills through a trail, through the lily pads. We looked over at this big stick of driftwood hanging at an angle out of the water, and there had to be ten or twelve baby ducks all in a row, all looking towards their left. I said, "Holy shit, for the first time in our lives, we've finally seen it – ducks in a row!" We have all heard that. And there they were. A bunch of ducks in a row, all looking in the exact same direction spaced evenly apart. I would give anything to have a picture of that.

***

IT'S EASY FOR ME to pick out my worst gig ever. Me and a bass player were placed in a band that was playing on the road. They had lost some members, and they were playing at the Imperial House in Dayton.

It was a band called September's May, and it was playing at the fabulous Boom Boom Room downstairs of the Imperial House. Probably one of the only cool things that happened there was that I met Dayton "Salt" Walther, the Indy car driver. He helped me with my pain of being in a band that sucked, and we drank a lot together. It was pretty cool to meet an Indy car driver, and he had been through a horrific crash. He took me to his Dayton "Salt" Walther Marina where he had his hydroplanes, his dragsters, his Indy cars and his Ferraris and all of his shit. He was a great guy.

Anyhow, this husband and wife team in the band dressed in formal attire. She always wore a gown, and he always wore a tuxedo. They faced each other and held hands and sang Neil Diamond shit. It was awful. One of the worst

Al thinking "just shoot me."

songs was a twenty-minute version of "Tie Me Kangaroo Down Sport" that we played because he was Australian.

All the drummer did on this song was click on the rim of the snare drum, click, click, click, to go with "tie me kangaroo down sport." Then he would say, "I want to tell a story." And I had to keep the little drum click going. He would talk about, oh, "The koala bear, everybody thinks the koala bear is such an innocent little guy, and he just sits up in the Eucalyptus trees and here the koala bears eating the eucalyptus, and it makes him high. He is just up there, high, waving his hand and just high as a kite, watching the world go by and the koala bear is quite happy."

I would look back at the bar manager in the back of the room; he would have his finger to his head like he was shooting himself and make his head go to the side. On break he would ask, "How in the hell do you do it? Every fucking night, how do you do it? Let's have a shot. You are a bigger man than me. Goddamn they suck." And a month of that was just brutal.

***

THEN I ENDED UP back in Columbus, and I got back with Bob Mohney and John Green. He was the manager of the Playboy Club at the Desert Inn. Probably Central Ohio's greatest show club was the Desert Inn. It was a true Las Vegas supper club; the acoustics were fabulous; the seating was fabulous; the bar back in the back was up high, and then it dropped low in the front with booths; it had a large stage, and right across the street was the Kahiki. You can get on the Internet and see it is still rated as one of the top ten restaurants to ever have been in America …the great Kahiki. Anyhow, the Desert Inn is gone now.

I got a call that a showband was in town, a band from Buffalo or something. Their drummer decided that he had had enough and called the sheriff. He wanted no problems, just wanted them to open the equipment trailer to get his clothes and his equipment and leave. Would I come out and play drums that night? I said why sure. So I got out to the club, and it was funny, anytime I went out there in Levis you couldn't get past the bunny at the long walkway to get into the club. But you could go to the left and go into the casual bar.

So I would always go to the casual bar and say hello and then walk through the corner of the kitchen out to the main room and drink with John. When I would leave, the bunny always wondered how in the hell I got in there with

Levis. But anyhow, I suppose this time I had a suit on. So I go sit at the bar. I had set my drums up. There was a group of three or four guys at the corner of the bar where I was sitting. They were pretty funny, and we talked a bit. The band was due to start in a couple of hours. John told them, "Al is in the band tonight with these guys."

They said, "What kind of stuff do you do?"

I said, "Hell, it beats the shit out of me; I haven't even met them."

In disbelief they said, "Well, how in the hell do you do that? Now we have got to stay and see how this works out."

The band came in and said, "Do you want to go to the dressing room and hear some tapes?"

I said, "Not at this point." You know, they were a showband, and I probably knew pretty much what they were going to do. If you did listen to the tapes, you would maybe try to remember something, that split second could screw you up – just go in shooting from the hip and just laying it out with your gut feeling. I just wanted to sit there until it was time to go up and play, and play without anything clogging my mind.

Sure enough it was a great band. They would play about a half a song and go to another one, play about half of the song, maybe twenty-five songs in a row. It turned out to be a fun night, and if I would have listened to the tapes, it wouldn't have helped.

It wasn't long after that our buddy Bill Kates, who was a booking agent and had played in a lot of trios and five piece bands, wanted to put a kick-ass showband together, a tribute to Lou Rawls. We did it at Damon's Den at the Continent up on 161. They had a big show club downstairs, a really big nice room.

During the week Tuesday through Thursday, it was a trio with Bob Mohney playing organ, Mike Beavers playing sax and me playing drums with Bill singing. We could do anything. Then on Friday and Saturday we brought in a horn section from Capital University, making it a nine or ten piece band, and we did the tribute to Lou Rawls, an hour and half show.

THE BILL KATES SHOW

The bartender said we quickly destroyed a bunch of great college kids with Amaretto slammers, Amaretto and a splash of soda in a rock glass with a napkin over it. You smacked it on the bar real hard and chugged it. We had a picture of all of us doing that, just to help the young guys realize what was ahead of them in the business. It was a lot of fun.

They all read music, I didn't. But with Mohney it was ok, I could read him like reading music. I could just tell if his head was cocked to the left, what he had in mind or where his great chords, octaves and notes were going to lead us. If he looked over a break in the song was coming; we pulled this shit off like we had been playing in Vegas for years.

We always met in the office off to the side and had a little pow wow, and broke like a pack of football players. The guy with the spotlight up in the top corner would put the light on the band walking to the stage, and we started this big fanfare prelude like Lou Rawls would do. Da, da da pause, da da da da. The tympani drums would roll, the spotlight would go to the corner where Bill Kates was coming out, and they would introduce him as an incredible Vegas star and lead him to the stage with the light. When he got up there, Mike Beavers, who was just the funniest son-of-a-bitch in the world, introduced him. Beav was another guy that reminded me of Dudley Moore, and he could be a mess; but when he got on stage, he was real crisp and clean in his tuxedo and spoke perfectly.

About then the movie *A Star is Born* came out with Kris Kristofferson and oh, what's her name, Barbara Streisand. Instead of introducing the incredible Bill Kates, Beav said, "Ladies and Gentlemen, I would like to introduce the incredible Esther Hoffman Howard." Just like they introduced her in *A Star is Born*, Oh my god.

Me and the organ player were all just in tears laughing. Bill was pissed, and we wanted to be slapping hands; it was so good. We all had to keep going because that was right when the intro busted in to "Groovy People."

One night my mom and dad were there. They just thought it was a great to see their kid in a big band doing all of these fancy arrangements. It was swinging; the room was alive; I looked out and mom and dad were enjoying it. My ex-wife and her friends were at another table and some friends from Delaware were at another. I had taken my girlfriend, Cathy, and she realized that it was kind of fucked up. She left, and that was my ride home.

We had an apartment in Delaware, up on the northwest side. I knew I was up shit creek. I didn't want to call anybody even though there was snow on the ground, so I just had another shot or two. I thought I will walk out of here; the worst that could happen is that I end up at the Ruckmore at 23 and the freeway. I will just stay there or something. I knew the manager, and I knew the owner lived there upstairs.

I didn't realize how damn far it would be to hop the fence and cross I-71, walk up clear around the ramp of I-270, west on I-270 in eight inches of snow in my little dress, pussy loafers. I walked about halfway to the Ruck, and I was freezing my ass off. A guy pulls over and picks me up and says that he just got off work at three a.m. in Columbus, and he lived in Marion.

He said he would take me home. He said, "I'm having a beer. Reach in the back I've got a six-pack there to get me to Marion." I got me a beer, and said you can just drop me off anywhere in downtown Delaware. I was happy to be that far, and was just going to walk to Hawk Road. He said, "Oh, no man. I'll run you all the way home."

Cathy was pissed that night. I wasn't too bummed. I was cold and wet, but I had a beer, and I got a ride home. I wasn't but a couple of hours behind her. That's just the way shit goes in a band. That's the way it went that night.

It had to be pretty soon after I met the bartender Karyol at the Gathering Inn in Delaware. The bar probably had about twelve bar stools, maybe the place held seventy people, a fireplace, a real kicked back, neat room. I was back with the Donnie Wilson Band and playing the great old stuff, and by god, I thought this bartender was pretty damn cute.

Bo Shall, a buddy of mine ran the bar, and I said to him, "Boy, I like her."

He said, "Well, she's not doing too good with her old man." So I just kept going in there. On my birthday I'm in there, she gave me a little pinch and said, "Happy birthday," with a smile. Oh my, the rest is history. People didn't think a bartender and a musician could hang together. It's been thirty-three years. I remember sometimes people would say to her, "How could you stand your old man being in a band?" Or some other people would say, "How do you stand your old lady being a bartender six nights a week?" I never worried about it. I said, "It never crossed my mind; I never worried about her."

She would say she didn't worry, "When they get off work at two in the morning, the band goes to a Waffle House or to their hotel room. There aren't any girls looking at them; I've seen them. When those guys are out of town, they get a hotel room. They've got a bottle of Cuervo, a case of Bud, a hundred chicken wings and a pizza. They don't much give a shit about anything else other than eating, drinking and watching MASH or Andy Griffith on the TV." And that's the way it went for many, many years.

A great moment with Karyol is when I got a cool call. I got to do a lot of neat things with the state fair, musically or helping with security with my background. I got the call to go down there, and it turned out I was working with Eddie Money. Karyol always told me she loved Eddie Money. I said, "Man, my girlfriend loves you, and this just happens to be her birthday."

He said, "Send a car for her, and get her down here." I walked her back to the trailer where Eddie was, but I didn't tell her what was going on. I said, "Well, give him a hug. Meet Eddie Money."

He went over and picked her up and said, "Happy birthday," and had her off the ground. He sang "Happy Birthday" to her, boy, you just can't beat stuff

Eddie Money and Karyol Roop

like that. It's one of my favorite pictures I have, Eddie in a black shirt and blue sports jacket, Karyol had on Levis and some kind of black bodysuit top.

***

THOSE DAYS STARTED a pretty cool thing. By now I'm not working in hotels, six nights a week. I had to take my equipment to each job every night we played. Sometimes it was on Sundays or Tuesdays or Friday and Saturday. I had a chance to do other jobs and had a limo, not to be used as a party car really; it was before they were used as party cars.

They were still celebrity cars. Sometimes they didn't want the limo; they wanted me to rent a car. I would go to Budget Rent-a-Car and get a black or dark grey Lincoln Town car and drive entertainers around for promoters I knew, because I was in the business, so they gave me the jobs.

I had a chance to go get Smokey Robinson and that turned into a pretty damn good friendship for several years. My buddy Dean Hughes worked security at the Bogey Inn and sometimes took animals on the David Letterman Show. Known as Big Dean Hughes, he looked like Mr. Clean and was strong as an ox and sharp as a tack.

He said, "Al, when we go to the theatre, or to the airport, let's wear grey pants, a white shirt, and blue blazer." He had a pair of sunglasses for me to match his.

He said, "This will look good to them. They like this kind of stuff."

We go out to the airport and Smokey comes in; he

knew we were probably there for him. And sure enough we were. We got him down to the Palace, and he put on a great show. While they were doing the show, the road manager and I would be the witness for counting the money because all these guys did cash. We would then go back to the hotel and make sure it was put in the safe.

Then back to the theatre and a lot of times we had to come up with decoys. Like that night it was cold, the guys said, "There are a lot of people waiting by the stage door to see Smokey. Let's come up with something different to get him out, so he won't stop and talk to people, get cold, and maybe sick. We will take Smokey up the aisle in the theatre which was empty, near doors to the east alley."

While the people were waiting for Smokey at the north alley, we ran the limo up the street, and went the wrong way in an alley, south toward Broad Street. Dean would jump out and knock on the door at the top of the theatre, and Smokey ran out with towels around him so he wouldn't get pneumonia or anything. He would get in the car and we were off. Diversions were a cool part of the job.

One of the neatest things was at the end of his show, Smokey got me and said, "Thanks for everything. Now I am going to walk across the front of the stage and greet people. And they will damn near pull me off." So he grabbed my belt in the back with his fist. He said, "You hold onto me by my belt real tight like that, and we will walk across the stage, and they won't pull me off."

So we walked across the stage, boy, they would tug on him, I was leaning my fat ass back, holding him by the back of his pants, holding him back, and we got across the stage. He told us we were his favorites after that. Many times, we passed on the limo and just rented a town car to go get him. That was quite a lot of fun working with a gentleman like him. One of the greatest guys I met in my life.

***

I LIVED PRETTY CLOSE to O'Charley's off Polaris, north of Columbus. The daytime bartender was a good friend. He knew I played for a living. There were some guys sitting at the bar, including this nice looking guy in a football jersey. They were eating some chicken wings and having a good time.

He said, "Man, these guys are in a band. They must be good. They have a big bus out back." He said come over and meet them. I later thought I bet that was about the last time this guy ever road a bus with a band, that he had his own Lear jet. I saw him on TV not too many months later; he had taken over the music scene. He was hosting award shows on TV. But there he was in Columbus and just a real guy, a hell of a nice guy. The guy's name is Usher!

***

ANOTHER ONE THAT AMAZED me happened at a bar at the Continent north of Columbus called R&R, Rock and Roll Bar. I worked a couple of jobs for them. They were having a meet and greet one night and limos were pulling in, and the radio gal I knew who was putting on the show put me in charge of Gene Simmons.

I thought that Gene was probably an outrageous guy, but I didn't have a clue. I just knew KISS was way out there. They weren't a band I followed, and I really didn't know much about Gene. He was in the back of the car, and I was in the front, and we were sitting by the rear door of R&R, out by the dumpsters. Nobody knew us or saw where we were; we were shooting the shit.

Gene was such a nice guy, like talking to my brother. He said, "Al, instead of sitting way up there, why don't you come back here and sit so you don't have to lean around the corner." So I sat in the middle seat, and we were shooting the shit until security came out and said it was time for Gene to go in. I suppose we sat there for at least a half-hour, and to my surprise, what a delightful guy he was to talk to! I sure enjoyed those moments with Gene. I will never in my life forget it.

***

AN ED MOMENT, HE knew I was up at St. Clair's house in Delaware. He was out riding around with his buddy Pat Melony and his pet coon Freddy. He couldn't keep Freddy out of his house so they became friends. He stayed on his shoulder or lap to Delaware for a visit then back to Clintonville, only Ed!

***

ANOTHER ONE I WILL never forget was when Dean Hughes and I went to the airport again. We were hired to pick up Jay Leno for the Palace Theatre; our connection was our buddy who owns Promo West and the Newport. We go to the airport, and again we are wearing our sunglasses and our grey slacks and waiting on Leno. He looks over at us, and I am not shitting you, the first thing to come out of Leno's mouth was, "Who the fuck is after me? The Ayatollah?"

We proceeded on to the limo that was right out front. My brother had said, "Hey if you get talking to Leno, ask him who the hell dresses Carson?"

So I said, "Jay, Ed wanted me to ask you, who dresses Carson?"

He replied, "I don't know, the fucker's from Nebraska."

That's all I got. We got down to the Palace and got him all situated. Somebody from the Newport knew Jay loved Lamborghinis and a friend of the owner, had a Lambo sitting outside the stage door. After the show, he offered to run over to the Newport and drive it on to the stage. The option was there if he wanted to ham it up, but Leno didn't take him up on that offer. But the guy who owned the Lamborghini was there and he said, "You know, since I have had it, the defrosters never worked."

He knew that Jay, before he was a comedian, worked on exotic cars in New York and Leno said, "Let me take a look at it." He took his sports jacket off and handed it to me. He got under the dash on the passenger side, then under the hood, and then got back under the dash, and finally said, "You got a defroster now." And by god, he did have a defroster. We couldn't believe it. Leno puts his coat back on, and says, "It's about time to go." And then he went in and did his big show at the Palace Theatre. Boy, what a guy!

When Dean and I were done with a limo job, we would stop for a Cuervo, and he would give his toast; I always liked to hear it. He would say, "These good ol' friends are hard to find, always keep it in your mind, when you find the ones that are true, don't forsake the old for the new."

***

IT WAS SO FUN working at the Palace. I must have worked twenty or more acts there. Once my commitment with the band was over, or until they were done, I could wander around anywhere. It was Smokey who had a party in the ballroom down underneath the theater. It was a gorgeous room with red carpet and the flocked wallpaper and chandeliers, a room that would hold a hundred people, I suppose.

They had bartenders and everything; it was a meet and greet room. Beside it, it had a kitchen that kind of looked like a naval ship or something with a gray painted floor. Along all of the hallways there were yellow, red and blue lines, all traveling upstairs in different directions. They would be marked "to stage left," or "to stage right, kitchen, green room." Stage right, if you were looking at the stage, would be on your left. That would let the performers know where their dressing room was or where their friends were in the greenroom. If they wanted to hit the kitchen, they could follow a color that went downstairs into the kitchen area.

There used to be a company called Concert Kitchens that did a lot of the shows. They would prepare food for these bands that had fifty to sixty people traveling with them, with stage crew and the truck and bus drivers, and they would prepare lunch and dinner for them. The next day again breakfast and lunch was served and the same until they got out of there. Man, they had kick-ass chicken noodle soup, chicken breasts, pork chops and fried potatoes, depending on who was there.

I loved to walk around the Palace. I found an area under the stage, where the big pipe organ was on a huge set of screws. There was a platform that held the organ. They would screw it up into the stage above, over from it on this big ramp that went down into like a two-car garage, all cement.

There used to be a lot of Barnum & Bailey circus stuff underneath, including a place to wash the elephants. They would walk them down this ramp into this huge area that was a shower area for circus animals. To see that and to hear the stories from guys that had worked at the theatre for forty years or so. These old boys that ran lighting or took care of the electric, were just unbelievable. They showed me secret passages and rooms where you could see the organ's big pipes. Up by the box seats there were doors that lead into the pipes that go up, I don't know, six or eight stories, into the office building there, the Laveck Tower. It was pretty amazing, the internal works.

When you came in the stage door, there was a green room with a couch, and there was a gal that sat in a booth. She had a bank of old round push button switches for the six or seven floors that went up the staircase right there beside her; they kind of spiraled up. Maybe there were four dressing rooms on each floor, and they had the little mosaic tile bathrooms, little carpeted rooms with a velvet love seat and a make-up mirror. She had buttons on the wall where she could give each individual room a five-minute warning bell and a one-minute warning bell, so you knew that it was time to come down the stairs and get into the green room so you could get on the stage cued-in on time. Just the internals of that building that had worked through vaudeville, Barnum & Bailey circuses and super stars over the years was amazing.

***

MY DAD WAS FROM German Village in Columbus, and like everybody, was broke back then. He knew the guy that ran the Palace Theater, and dad in his teens would do caricatures and portraits of people who performed there that were just unbelievable. I've got originals he did of Cab Calloway, Clark Gable, Sid Caesar, and I just can't think of them all. Back in those days for the theatre to have photographs done was expensive and not that easy, so dad

Rusty Bryant

did a lot of drawings for people that were coming to the Palace and they made posters out of them for their marquees.

I have a beautiful pencil drawing of Red Skelton that was signed "Nate Roop" with whatever date on it. I used my connections and said to security, "I've got this picture of Red that my dad did."

They said, "Well, let's see if we can't get you in to see Red." And there he was, in all his glory, the fabulous smile of Red Skelton in his tuxedo and his fancy show shoes with the black bows on them. I said to him, "My dad drew your picture quite some time ago when you were at the Palace Theatre, and I wanted to see if I might get it autographed."

He wrote on it, "Dear Nate, my thanks, I'm grateful for the copy I received of your artwork and wish you all the best, Red." I was able to give that to Dad in his later years, which was cool. I was always a big Red Skelton fan and obviously still am.

***

AROUND 1989 DAVE ST. CLAIR and I went Atlantic City for a limo show. My buddy Moon was driving us to Crestline, Ohio to catch the train. Out in the middle of nowhere, well north of Delaware, the left front wheel of the limo fell off. This is probably eleven or twelve at night, with little time to spare. I went up to a house, showed the guy my car and told him about the train. I made him an offer to get us to Crestline, and he said ok. Moon had to wait for a tow truck, and made sure it was back on the road in a few days to pick us up.

On the train out of New York headed home, we were standing at the bar drinking with a well dressed very nice guy who turned out to be the great composer Marvin Hamlisch, also headed for Columbus, by way of Crestline.

He told great stories and jokes, a very fun person. He would say let's have more wine, and we said sure. Someone asked him how he would get from Crestline to Columbus, he said, "I have a limo waiting for me." He looks at me and Dave and asks, "How do you guys get to Delaware?"

We said we have a limo, and he slapped his hand down and said, "You guys are so funny, let's get another bottle of wine."

At two in the morning we pull into the station that is only a parking lot, and there are two limos backed in side by side. We're looking over the roof of Marvin's limo; I think his jaw was hanging down, in shock. In our old Levis we said thanks and goodbye. Off we went with are buddy Moon driving. We had a blast telling Moon the story. Moon drove that car for years.

***

I WAS THINKING BACK about the seventies when I was out in Denver, when I wasn't working or when we were between bands, I discovered a place I liked, more of a towny bar, more toward downtown called the Tiger's Lair. The house band there was Glass Menagerie. I somehow remember a guy's name was Persell who was in the band; I think he was the leader and sax player. I was in there one day checking it out and a cute little bartender said, "How are you doing? How's everything?"

I said, "Fine I'll have a Bud."

She was eating a Hershey bar she said, "You look like you could use part of this." So she broke off about a third of her Hershey for me. I had that to go with my beer and, she was nice to talk to. She said, "Where are you from?"

I said, "Ohio. I came out here to play."

Here's what a small world it is, she said, "Oh, did you come out with Bob Mohney?"

And I said, "Yeah." So we shot the shit a little bit and I thought, oh my gosh, this is a cute gal, and she shared her candy bar with me. I was hoping maybe I wouldn't be sleeping in my van that night. I somehow ended up leaving. I ran into Mohney a day or two later when we were at a job and I said, "My god, I was down at the Tiger's Lair and met a cute gal. She figured I was in town with you."

He said, "I bet the guy in the band was watching you, because that's his ol' lady." He was the leader of Glass Menagerie. It was a kick-ass band and anyhow that gal who was so nice never told me that she was with the guy in the band. Mohney said I was lucky, if I would have stayed around, he would have beat the shit out of me; that's the way he was. Just another weird moment in Denver, Colorado.

***

PROBABLY THE LAST of the seventies' craziness was with a guy named Bob Hutchison. He had a beauty salon called Inner Visions up on Henderson. He and his staff drank at the Studio 5 and was part of the gang there that we had so much fun with. He called me one day and he said, "Come up here." They were just getting into painting hair, which is kind of putting blonde highlights in it. And he said, "Come up, we want you to be the first one we paint. We got a bottle of Tequila, so just come up here and have a couple of shots and let us experiment on you with putting foil on you and painting your hair."

So I did, and they became really good friends, and it turns out they knew how to really throw parties. Between Bob Hutchinson who owned the shop and our really good friend Mary, Proud Mary, she kind of reminded me a little bit of Maude on the TV show, naughty Maude. She had a dry, great humor, and she was just crazier than shit. She decided to throw a party for Bob.

But first, it's Bob who throws a party for everybody in his salon at his house over on the Scioto River Road. It was a scavenger hunt party. This is how crazy these people were at Studio 5, the regulars. We all go to this beautiful home, and he had a punch everybody had to drink to make sure he got you real buzzed up. It then became a scavenger hunt, and everybody was in different cars.

Only the driver of the car knew that there was a tape recorder to record the conversation in the cars. And everybody thought they would go with the people they came to the party with, but that changed when Bob gave the rules.

With Polaroid camera in hand it was time to go out and get the most creative picture at a bar, in a bathroom at a bar, over by the zoo, oh, the criteria was pretty unbelievable. You had a list to do, and nobody knew that it was being recorded. Bob selected who went with who, and he split-up everybody. You didn't go with your spouse or whom you came to the party with.

There were conversations on the recording like, "Hey, Jimmy isn't here, come over here." "Sit on my lap." "Show me your tits." "Get your hand off of my ass." "Here, I will sit on you, Brian, if you feel happy I'm sitting on you." And "Jane, you have nice panties, better than my wife, Oh, this is great." The cars were packed full of people that were all juiced up and feeling a little naughty. The conversations were great and being recorded, and they did all of their tasks which included the best mooning pyramid in front of the zoo, or the best bathroom picture at the Wyandott Inn or something, and the conversations just got naughtier and naughtier in the car.

When they all got back to Bob's house for the party, he took all of those tapes and set his sound system up on the balcony and played all of them. It started with somebody saying, "It's a good thing Bill isn't here with your hands on my tits." It was a great screw-over to hear the tapes back at the party and see the pictures they took with the Polaroids.

To get even, my buddy Proud Mary put together a party to screw Bob. They threw a party at a party house at Reid and Henderson, A "You're a sucker, This Is Your Life party."

It was supposed to be a come the way Bob's wife caught you over the last couple of weeks party. I had, of course, rode the little mini-bike through Studio 5 naked, so Bob thought I would at least be there in nothing more than underwear. His wife had leggings on and a little short top (which she quickly changed). Bob was in his white underwear because that's the way he was supposed to come. You were supposed to go to the party the way you were spotted. At the party there were these big huge suckers hanging from all of the lights in this party house. The cake was a big sucker.

Bob was the real sucker; he was the only one in underwear. When he opened the door up, everybody else was in sport jackets and nice slacks. He tried but couldn't get away. They threw him into the room, so he just posed like muscle man and strolled his skinny ass around the room; it was beautiful. They said, "Bob this is your life!," like the old TV show "This is Your Life." They put him in his chair, and said, "Bob, here are a few of your beauticians who won competitions in Chicago." They came out, and they had bones in their hair like Pebbles in the Flintstones and had goofy hairdos. They then said, "Bob, here's your lawyer."

He came out and said, "Bob, I didn't know your life was going to turn to shit, or I wouldn't have represented you."

Then from behind the curtain was another voice, "Bob, when you were a child, you were such a good boy."

And they said, "That's right Bob. That's your beautiful mother. She said I didn't know you would turn into such a piece of shit." She came out, and here is poor Bob in his white underwear. Everyone from Upper Arlington is there, everybody from his salon, his customers, hair dressers, people who he had won competitions with, his lawyer, and his mother; everybody was there, and they present him his book, "This is Your Life, Bob Hutchison." It was just a tremendous screw-over party. It was just too damn much fun, and that's how they got even with him for his party.

Harold Smith

***

IN THE EIGHTIES, I LOVED playing with Harold Smith. He played down around Long Street, Spring Street, and Allegheny Avenue. He called himself "Number One Guitar." Boy, he could play just like Wes Montgomery. He had such a good band. I played with him with Bob Mohney playing organ; we had a trio. And for a while it was Harold Smith, Bob, Flip Jackson and me at Brothers.

It was at 792 East Long Street, just east of the freeway, there was a neighborhood bar downstairs and upstairs, a jazz or blues club. We were playing there five nights a week: Wednesday, Thursday, Friday, Saturday and Sunday. We were there for four or five months a couple of times. It was one of the greatest jobs I ever had.

Boy, Harold, when he would fire up, playing something like Wes Montgomery's "Bumpin' on the Sunset," it was a big groove, and it might go for fifteen or twenty minutes. He would stop in the middle of it and say, "We need some gin up in here. Could we get some gin? Pantyhose will be flying." Colt 45s and shots of gin would come up to the stage; it was absolutely incredible.

Flip, originally was with the Eddie Kendricks Band, arranged the horn stuff, and they did the song "Keep on Truckin." That was a hell of a band; Flip ended up married to Martha Reeves, of Martha Reeves and the Vandellas. They had a home in Detroit.

I was drinking with Flip one day and he said, "Well, I fucked that up. Now I don't have a big home with a swimming pool in Detroit." But my god, the music up there at my brother's place with Number One Guitar Harold Smith and Flip from the Kendricks Band was unbelievable.

One night we got off work and had some drinks. The bar had closed, but we still had access because we had not left yet. We were sitting on the staircase, on the second floor over Long Street, and you could hear the cars on Route 70 in front of us, probably I-71 to the right of us, and on Long Street you could hear people talking shit and taxicabs just local neighborhood in the middle of the night stuff.

We sat out there enjoying the world, and Flip had some stories. I wish I could remember them as he told them. He was telling me about the mathematics of music, and what key was most appealing to everybody to begin with. Mathematically B flat is the most common thing to our ears, like the sounds we were hearing, the sounds of the city, the sounds of the trucks going by, and the people talking, murmuring out on the street. Together all of the sounds of the city are B flat so that is the most common thing to your ear, and he was telling me mathematically why a lot of his sax solos are in B flat because its already the most familiar to your ears and pleasing to you.

Even down to the point that breaking wind, the all-American fart, is basically B flat. The great song "Misty," is B flat. So many things are B flat, and his mathematics story of why people write or play in B flat was phenomenal. If it is already the most common, acceptable thing to your ears, you are going to appreciate what you are hearing. So if you write a song, do it in B flat.

It was just amazing to talk to Flip out there. By the time we were finishing, you could hear birds chirping, daybreak was starting to come, and we were still sitting on this shit-hole fire escape at my brother's place on Long Street. But to hear a talent like Flip explain music was just phenomenal.

***

MOHNEY AND I HAD BEEN working at the Sheraton North on 161 as a trio with Deborah Randall singing, and Bob with his Hammond, a kick-ass trio. Deborah Randall could smoke on stuff like the "Lady is a Tramp" and "Candy Kisses for the Love." It was a really, really a hot band, doing standards and current stuff. We had an opportunity to go to Baltimore to the Sheraton there. They had just recently re-done their riverfront district down there, and the Sheraton was connected to the Mechanic's Theatre, which is pretty cool. When we were there, Bob Fosse's Dancin' was the theatre act there. After their show, the horn players would come in and play with us.

Leaving Mohney's house on 161, trying to get the organ down the staircase, we ended up sliding down the staircase with it. Bob said, "Well, shit, we'll see if it starts when we get there." B-3s are temperamental, but we got down there, and it was ok.

We were un-
loading our stuff
and they said,
"Whoa, you can't;
we're union; you
can't touch your
equipment. We'll
get it upstairs to
the twentieth floor
nightclub for you."
They asked us if we
had our card. We
were all members
of Columbus Fed-
eration of Musi-
cians, Local Union
at one time. I think

the last endorsement on my card was in 1978 or something. I still had my
card and showed it to them and they didn't turn it over to see the dates. They
said, "Fine, your equipment will be upstairs." It was a great job.

We met the guys that were playing in the Mechanic's Theatre from Bob
Fosse's *Dancin'*. We would be playing around midnight when their show was
over. They would hear what song we were playing, and you could hear the sax
player and the trombone player picking up on what we were playing coming
down the hallway. They would come in and join us for the last set of the night.
It's hard to believe that could happen, but it did.

We didn't know it before we got there, but Bob and I got stuck with a cocktail hour set. The normal band gig was from nine to one in the morning, but
we also had to do five to seven cocktail hour, just Bob and me. Luckily, they
had a guy there cutting big medium rare prime rib with little rolls and some
other stuff. He knew that we didn't bargain for that extra playing, so he would

cut-off about five inches of that prime rib from the butt end and slide it under my floor tom drum, by my right leg. He would put a napkin over it. We would have equal to about four prime rib dinners, which we could take to our room every night. That's one of the little perks you get when you get in with the bar and food staff. So we had to play the little cocktail hour thing, maybe Tuesday,

Wednesday, Thursday and Friday, but they took good care of us.

We had rooms on the third floor. We had sliding doors like all of them, but ours were not the best rooms. They weren't out on a patio looking out over Baltimore. They went out onto the roof; there was the banquet room under us, so it was just a gravel roof.

We would go out there at night and take our chairs, and across the street was a place similar to a White Castle. They had small burgers, and one night we saw some guys down there, and we thought about burgers. We were up there having a beer on the roof at two in the morning. We said, "If we drop you down some money, will you get us a dozen of those little greasy burgers with onions?"

And they said, "Yeah." We cracked up. There were probably six in a bag. They would throw the wrapped up bag, but it wouldn't quite get up the building and fall back down. They would throw them again, eventually we would get them after they bounced off the building a few times. We got our burgers, and they got a tip. We sat up there on the roof and had a damn good time.

One night we were sitting up there, looking out over the city on this gravel roof, and we heard somebody yell, "Hey, Roop." We looked down, and there was a white cargo van turning the corner. It was Mark Cornelius, a friend from Columbus, hanging out the window looking up at us. He dated the girl in our band. He had been playing on the coast somewhere; his gig was over, and he comes up to Baltimore and finds the Sheraton. In the middle of the night, happened to see us on the edge of the roof maybe because those guys were throwing us burgers or whatever. I can't remember, but he yelled up at us.

What's the chances in Baltimore, Maryland, our singer Deborah's boyfriend rolls into town, and yells up from the corner? Oh, that was just another good night.

The same band, me, Bob, and Deborah, were at the Sheraton North for a while. Over the years I played there in the band called "Flashback," and Mimi Russo played there with her lounge band before she got into Spittin' Image and really kicked ass. It was remodeled and it was Bob, Deborah and myself

Al, Deborah and Mohney

back again. In all of the hotel bands we sometimes changed the words like the song "Lyin' Eyes" we would sing, "She woke up and got herself a stiff one." There were many changes we made on "Crocodile Rock." Usually only regulars or bartenders caught it. Some songs we had to make up words because we didn't know what the hell they were saying. Sister Golden Hair's song at the end we kept saying, 'raul bop funeman, raul bop funeman,' and it worked.

The state fairgrounds still had their bands outside. And one night Willie Nelson had been at the fairgrounds, and he walked in the lounge at the Sheraton north with his crew. So here comes Willie. He walks in the door and Bob Mohney, being the genius organ player he was, switches from whatever the melody we were playing to a Willie Nelson melody.

Willie came over and just leaned on the organ top with his arms folded and said, "Play another one for me." Bob, of course, played a short medley of his songs; it was a big hit.

His horn player, Joe Truly was his name, was anxious to play something besides what he played with Willie. He was a kick-ass sax player, a crazy guy.

By now it's about one in the morning, the last set. Joe sat in with us, and he did a song called, I don't know what it was called, but it was, "baby, oh baby, you're drinking too much, I'm afraid you might drown, I'm just your money clown." Slow dirty blues.

And as it turns out, Willie was so knocked out with Mohney, he flew him out to Las Vegas a couple of times to play. One night we were playing at the Sheraton downtown, and Mohney was going to be a little late getting there because he was in Las Vegas doing a show with Willie. But he got there, and gave me and Donnie Wilson about a half-dozen silver dollars each from the casino he had been in with Willie, and a nice thank you note from Willie. It was hard to believe from the Sheraton on 161 to Willie and Joe Truly.

Their semi driver had their trailer at the fairgrounds, but their truck was beside the Sheraton. I said, "Well, we can walk over to the Blarney Stone and have a nightcap, next door."

He said, "Hell no. We got the truck and driver right here." We drove next door to the Blarney Stone and had a couple of drinks. My god did we love getting to do something with Willie. He liked Mohney doing a song called "City." Two nights in a row they were there, I don't know who did "City" originally, but we did it for Willie several times, a good time at the ol' Sheraton.

***

YOU KNOW, HAVING a band back then was one thing. It was great to be with guys you knew, like Mohney, Mike Flore or Don Beck, and be in a band like Flashback or the Donnie Wilson Band. But every once in awhile in between jobs agencies would put you with a band. I worked with Summit Enterprises off of Oakland Park, and they would place you with bands. That's how I got placed with "What was the worst gig ever?" That was definitely a band I was placed in. But sometimes you had to do what you had to do. Being placed in a band, versus being in a band with people you knew and liked, was very different.

If a band was coming through town, and they needed a drummer, an agency like Summit Enterprises or Bill Kates could find someone. A hotel lounge band might need a bass man, and the agency might call you. Then you go meet these guys, and you learn their shit, which might be "Midnight Blue" or "Midnight at the Oasis" whatever it took. But boy, it was sure a lot nicer to play with guys you knew, that were playing music you liked. But it didn't work like that all of the time.

Ah, being in bands with friends makes me think of guys like Otis, Daryl Smith who moved from Columbus to Delaware, just like myself. I loved to work with him. He works in my buddy's band Rolly Gaumer and the Leftovers, called the Leftovers because it was part of the Barrel House, part Rolly Gaumer Band, part Rolling Hams, and part Dick Jackson and Country Sunshine. The leftovers, we all loved working together.

Otis, besides being able to sing Stevie Ray or Buddy Miles, the way he could do old soul songs was incredible. He could sing Marvin Gaye's song "Mother, Mother."

Oddly enough, again, what a small world it is, when I played in the band JJ that broke up in the seventies because Dale ended up with Rossington Collins, and to this day she is a member of Lynyrd Skynyrd, a great singer. Otis worked with their drummer that lived through the plane crash, Artimus Pyle. Occasionally, he would go to the east coast and work with the Artimus Pyle Band.

My buddy Flip Jackson, who I worked with on Long St. at Brothers, ended up having a band called Flip Jackson's Variations. He hired Bob Mohney on organ and me to play. We were the house band at the Embassy Suites on Cleveland Avenue. We had to wear tuxedos, and we weren't supposed to drink, but we had coffee cups once we knew the bartenders. The jazz radio station back then was Jazz 104, WBBY, and we were the WBBY band at Embassy Suites. We were there four or five months. My god, it was great, very few vocals, just a great organ, sax and drums band.

My car back then was an old piece of shit, an MGB GT. I would be sitting

Flip Jackson

at Embassy after work, and Mohney would say, "If you are going Roop, come on. I'm leaving now." My piece of shit would never start, so I would leave when Mohney left so he could push me out of the parking lot down Cooper Road, then I could take Cleveland Avenue home. You got to do what you got to do. We had a lot fun.

***

ED AND I USED to go to a couple of places through there to eat and have a drink. I was behind Ed in his Cutlass and me in that damn MG. He came up to Cleveland Avenue at the 161-turn lane; I couldn't stop, and I hit him; I hit him pretty damn hard. Hit hard enough that my left headlight was angled towards the ground. But Ed and his dry sense of humor, he acted like nothing happened. I knocked the shit out of him, really. On the left front of my car the fender and the headlight were demolished. I saw that he wasn't doing anything, so I didn't do anything. He didn't even look in his mirror. We were both glancing around at the people in the crosswalks, on the corners and at the gas station were looking. They were probably wondering, "Why don't these guys care? They just had a pretty significant crash."

And we just never did anything. Ed went on, and I went on like nothing happened. We got up to the road to the bar that we were going to, and then we looked at the cars. We drilled two holes in the fender of my MG and put a muffler clamp through it, a U-shaped clamp and put a chain on that and wrapped it around a pole at the bar we were at. I just kept backing up real hard until I pulled the fender out and the headlight went from shining toward the ground to back up where it should be. We thought, "Let's have a Jaeger and call it a day." That worked nice.

***

I WAS LUCKY to have connections with the State Fairgrounds. I was doing real limousine work, not just taking bachelor parties out or people out drinking. One of my jobs was strange at first, but ended very cool. New Kids on the Block were in town, and they were at a hotel downtown. There had been a rain delay. Tiffany and her bus were already up there and playing. They would send me down for New Kids in my limo with their manager, I forgot his name, maybe Biscuit, a great guy. To kill time we would take two or three at time to the mall because they liked to look for tennis shoes. I looked around, and nobody knew who anybody was.

I would go back to the fairgrounds and they would tell me, "Oh, not yet, not yet." Tiffany was still playing and her bus was there. I would go back downtown to the hotel, and sure enough, they were ready to go by then, no rain. But the natives were getting restless up there at the fair waiting for them. Some fans were hurt from pushing and shoving. Just like with the Beach Boys we had to do a lot of diversions.

We had to think about this so the band was put in the hotel van, with just the manager and me in the limo. Nobody was looking at the van, and it got right in. We got up to 17th Avenue; the van went on in; the State Patrol walked with the limousine, like in a movie with a King, and there wasn't anybody in the limo. But we got in backstage, got the car parked and figured out what to do. New Kids on the Block got to do their show, and the way they worked it out was Tiffany and her band took the hotel van back to the hotel. They left their bus there. And when New Kids on the Block were done, the crowd thought they would get into the limo.

We had told them no; there is no reason to wait; they are not coming; this was hundreds of people still watching the limo. The guys got on Tiffany's bus and went out undetected, because that bus had been there all day. That was one of the decoys, the crowd waiting, still saying "Oh, you're bullshitting us. They are still here; they are still here; because we saw you come in, blah, blah, blah." Me and the manager said again that they're gone; it's just us two.

And then a half hour later, when me and the manager went to leave, we got into the limo, and they were cursing us and giving us the finger. We said, "We told you." We just wanted to get back to the hotel, where all their busses were.

***

I HAVE AN ED MOMENT. The last Ed moment was hitting his car in the ass. This Ed moment was a dandy. Talking about life as a musician, Ed moments have to be there. Ed and I tried to plan to be at our parents' house on holidays at exactly the same time. So if Ed said he would be there at two p.m., I would be there at two p.m., and we'd walk in together.

He was my big six foot four two hundred seventy pound brother. He walks in the garage door into the kitchen and living room. Mom was in the kitchen. Dad was in his chair in the living room, and Dad drops his paper down and says, "Hello fellas."

Big ol' teddy bear Ed was walking through the living room saying, "Hi," and I see a bag drop on the ground. A plastic bag with green shit in it. So I put my foot on it before Dad sees it, and I pick it up and put it in my pocket.

Ed says, "Hi!" to mom and then I go over and catch Ed.

I said, "Ed, you dropped this, looks like pot in it. Here."

And he said, "I don't want that, Al. I don't want that. Dad, look what Al is trying to give me. Now, I don't mess with pot."

I was standing there holding a bag. I thought, wow I covered for him, but here was Ed's sense of humor; he dropped it knowing I would probably cover for him.

And as it turns out he said, "Al, that's a bag of catnip I got for mom."
SPEAKING OF ED STORIES, this is one I didn't think I would put in the book, but I will, because Ed's favorite musicians are in the story, and music is what this book is about.

He got sick, I guess it was early 2007, and not long after, dementia was setting in. I would go down to see him at the bar in Columbus and I thought, man he is getting real buzzed up early. So I went down earlier the next time, and he had just left his house and got there. I thought man, he hadn't had a drop, but he still is out there a bit.

That's when I realized the reason he had lost so much weight. Ed and I never talked about bad stuff. Even after I knew he was sick, we didn't discuss it. But the music part of it is I would go in and Ed would get a vodka, and he would say, "Oh, Al, you wouldn't believe it. Last night, we had a hell of a party. It was Elton John and Billy Joel, oh my gosh, goddamn, we had more fun."

And he was going on, "Goddamn, Elton and Billy, we had just a great time."

And another time I would go down there, and he would say, "Geez, me and Elton and Clapton had a party last night. I have to tell you that Eric Clapton is the most fun guy I ever partied with in my life."

And then he would just talk completely normal, and I would kind of beat around the bush, I would say, "Did you really party with Clapton last night?"

He said, "Al, boy, you would like to." And then a little while later he would say, "Geez, the fun Elton and me and Clapton had last night." Ed passed in his sleep in about six months. Apparently the dementia wasn't too bad to him.

We never did ever talk about anything bad, like are you mad at the folks or are you mad at me? We were never, ever mad at each other. And he chose, I'm sure not to tell me what was wrong.

Other people said, "What's wrong with Eddie?" We all knew something was bad, one day at the bar we were at a girl said to Ed, "Did you tell Al what you wanted to tell him?"

And he said, "Oh yeah, let's get this out of the way…I just wanted to tell you I love you." He paused and said, "Well actually, I love you like a brother." That was true Ed humor, and I never saw him again.

I went down to move his car at his house, another musical thing happened that was pretty cool. When I started his car, it was the *Best of Van Morrison*, so his last recollection was definitely Elton John, Eric Clapton, Billy Joel and Van Morrison. I still have it in my car. That's pretty cool shit. God bless you Eddie.

We've had wonderful musicians in our lives. When dad passed during his service, Rusty Bryant and Chuz Alfred walked in playing "Danny Boy" on their tenor saxes. When they finished, they put their horns by dad, and said, "This ole' boy wasn't going anywhere until we blew for him one more time." At mom's service, fifteen years later, Arnett Howard came in playing a soft song, walked up to mom and sang "The Final Mile" to her. For Ed, of course, it was our friend Willie Pooch who came in with a song. We thank them very much.

***

HOT DAMN! LIFE BROUGHT change in 1989 when I was asked to join the Great Barrel House Blues Band. We called it Bar Rock'en Blues. That's when you were playing at the Short North Tavern one night, in Gahanna one night, the Bogey, Backstretch, Red White and Boom, a different place the next night. Probably some of my favorite times I ever had in my life.

Billy had the Barrel House Band for many years with guys he went to school with and just prior to me being with them. It was Bill Bostwick playing guitar, Rolly Gummar playing bass, and Billy Simpson playing drums and singing all of the songs as a trio.

But Billy wanted to go all out, and he hired me to play drums, so he could go up front. I used to love to sit in and play drums with him. Billy and I battled each other for the best of shuffles, and I think we were neck and neck with the art of playing a badass shuffle. I was honored. Sometimes he would be playing, and I would walk in, and I would grab another set of sticks off the floor or wherever and lean over his shoulders and start playing with him, and it would be two guys playing one set of drums. We had more fun doing

BARREL HOUSE BLUES BAND

PRESENTED BY
Budweiser.
614-389-1110

that kind of shit. He hired me playing drums, George McDonald and Tommy Carroll were the guitar players, and Rolly was still the bass player. It was a kick-ass band.

Not too long after that we were lucky enough to get represented by Budweiser. Some people said, "Well, what does that do?" Oh, they bought us our shirts and custom jackets, table tents, and our posters were kick-ass. Twice a year our wives got brochures they could order from. And it gave the band some credibility; we looked good, and we were proud.

When we were working with B.B. King, he was with Budweiser also and since we were with Budweiser, we got to have an equal spot in the *Columbus Dispatch*. We got to have the Bud bow tie logo on our shirts. We did the Bud events at ski lodges and balloon festivals; and when the Budweiser girls were there, we would share the stage with them and treat them graciously, and boy it was great.

Billy Simpson is the most soulful blues guy out there. If you heard him on a tape you would have thought he was a brother, what a blues man he is. We

were playing at Newport, and he told B.B. King we were a R & B band.

B.B. said, "You're a blues band," and that's when we changed the name. That was pretty cool; I was standing right beside him.

The Barrel House Band went on doing five to six nights a week, sometimes twice a day. We might do the Rhythm and Food Festival in Columbus and then be at the Bogey that night. We gave it hell for about sixteen years. It was just unbelievable.

Another fun thing about the Barrel House Band was on New Year's Eve, it

was Tommy's birthday before midnight and George's after midnight.

The band was a traditional blues band, but we had really great arrangements. Nobody else was doing Tinsley Ellis, and Gary Moore had just done the album "Still Got the Blues." The Kinsey Report was one of my favorites. Stevie Ray Vaughan was at the top of his game and, we did a wide variety of his stuff like "Cold Shot" and some others.

But probably one of the neatest things, musically, in my life was being with a band that was so good you could really do Stevie Ray Vaughan's "Couldn't Stand the Weather" and nail it. That's a badass song to pull off. Every night that we did "Couldn't Stand the Weather" was a special tribute to the guys in his band, and our memories of Stevie Ray.

Another one we loved was Buddy Miles; he was kick-ass along with Savoy Brown, Albert King, and, of course, all of the Allman Brothers stuff. "Trouble No More" was a great song. Billy would tell everybody, "Well, here's one for you because here's what you will be doing tomorrow since you have been out

to hear the Barrel House Band." He would do "Call My Job Cause I Won't Be In Tomorrow." That was a big crowd pleaser.

One of the greatest tunes we did, so many people did it, but we did Billy's version of "Stormy Monday." And that was a hit. I'll tell you, the Donnie Wilson Band had "I Stand Accused" and the Barrel House Band had Billy Simpson doing "Stormy Monday." His version, toward the end of the song he would do a break and yell out, "I'm looking over here," and the band would go "bam;" "I'm looking over there," and the band would go "bam;" "I'm looking back there," and the band would go "bam." And then he would go into his speech, a rap about that sexy sassy look on your face, on & on, something I can't remember. He would get down to the end of it, and he would say, "You take care of my hot dog, I'll take care of your bun." The band finished it out and, oh boy, the crowd would go wild.

I was trying to think, Rolly was the bass player and then Scott Bock was the bass player for a little while. Then Tony Stidham was the bass player.

We were lucky enough to play at the Beer Barrel Saloon at Put-in-Bay, which is quite an honor. You know it's the biggest bar up there, maybe one of the biggest bars in the country. Playing there was great. We were there for three days, we had a condo to stay in and, of course, Billy was one of the features at the condo. He was blessed in the pri-

vates department. We were up there in the condo, and we had our wives with us because it was so cool, except when Billy had his loose little shorts on.

One thing I learned is when you play a matinee, got a break, then you play again at night, and do a matinee the next day, play that night, then on Sunday; it's a bitch. Even if you go fishing in between sets or have a few beers at the condo in between, it's a bitch.

One of my favorite nights was with George McDonald. While we were playing up in Catawba, it was just a short walk across the parking lot to be on the huge boulders, each the size of a car, by where the ferry goes out to Put-In-Bay. The Hale-Bopp Comet was going by then. We took a cooler out there and sat on those rocks, it was just so dark and beautiful over Lake Erie.

The stars and the Hale-Bopp Comet stretched across the sky. Being in a band is a lot of work, and a lot of hours, but when stuff like that comes along, you get to enjoy the sky over a lake at three or four in the morning with a buddy, and that's cool shit.

Speaking of George, we were at Buckeye Lake at the Paddle Wheel, right downtown before some of the new places came along. They said, "You can stay upstairs." We went up there and saw half-filled skillets full of grease and shit where other bands had been there. It was just trashed with a broken couch, a real dump. We went ahead and got hotel rooms out by the freeway.

It turned out to be a good gig. George's wife had put a little cooler together for George; it had some miscellaneous beers in it like Miller and PBR, some

Newport Music Hall

fried chicken, and George had his worms in there. When we got off work, we went over and sat on the bank of Buckeye Lake and fished a little bit.

The ice was gone; the beer was warm and kind of smelled like dirt and fishing worms, and so did the chicken. But in the middle of the night after you are done with a gig, you can't put a price on a night like that. You've got the world by the balls.

One time we had been the opening act for B.B. King at the Newport.

They liked us because we weren't hard to work with. We weren't demanding about how the PA sounded. We would get our stuff set up in front of B.B.'s stuff, and we would do our show, then peel it off the stage.

For the second set we would put our stuff back and do forty minutes before B.B. again. The stagehands liked us, and B.B.'s band liked us because we didn't have an ego, and we made it easy.

One time with B.B. we had played the opener, and we went to the dressing room. About fifteen minutes later B.B.'s bass player and keyboard man came in and stuck a hundred dollar bill in my hand with a shake. They said their drummer was stuck at an airport, and they said it would be a big favor if I would please play with them. I just about shit. I was never going to spend that bill, but on the way home we stopped at a bar at Graceland Shopping Center, and I blew it buying us shots on B.B. King.

A friend of Scott that owns the Newport, his buddy Ron Tibner, was there and liked the band really well, and he was about to get married. Ron was the personal manager for Ron Woods of the Rolling Stones for about twenty years. He asked us to play his wedding at the Newport.

We were honored to play their wedding. If you have ever been to the Newport, it's an old college bar, not real pretty, but a nice theatre that probably holds about a thousand people. They transformed it into a beautiful wedding site. They put maybe a 30x30 square foot screen behind the band to show fireworks because they met at Cincinnati during one of their big events during the fireworks.

Our equipment was set up and covered with white cloth, so you couldn't see it, and the whole stage was white with an elegant staircase going up to the stage from the main floor with enormous candelabras that this big place didn't dwarf. They were huge and they had closed off the balcony with like silk.

It was a gorgeous room for the wedding, with the wedding and the fireworks on the big screen. Ron and his wife had rented my limo to go to Gatlinburg for a week with my buddy Matt Puttuck, "Moon," another one of my best friends, driving. It was very difficult to back in, past the dumpster and turn the corner to get the limo on the stage, but after the Barrel House played this beautiful wedding, Moon pulls the limo right on the stage to pick up Ron and his wife and take them to Gatlinburg for a week. Moon was their driver for the week in Gatlinburg; that just had to be something.

Watching this wedding we all had goose bumps and lumps in our throats. It was probably one of the coolest I ever saw. I almost forgot a special part of the day. When Ron booked the job Billy Simpson said, "I won't forget that

date because it's my birthday." As busy as Ron must
have been, he remembered
to put a birthday cake and
Stroh's beer for Billy in our
dressing room.

***

THE BARREL HOUSE BAND
was certainly something. I
think it started in 1989 and
went for sixteen or seventeen years. Another good gig
was in a beautiful town called
Yellow Springs, out near
Springfield, kind of a hippie
town. We worked there in a
neat little pizza place blues
club. Down the road was a

Billy Simpson

small mom and pop hotel. We would all fit, we took the mattresses off the
two queen-sized beds and put them on the floor. We had a bottle of Jim Beam
a case of Bud, pizza and some chicken wings, and that's just all the hell you
need when you get off of work in a town like Yellow Springs.

Another one was in Gambier at Kenyon College. We played a fundraiser
they had on campus for the tropical rainforest. They had this big ballroom
we were playing in, and they had streamers blowing up from underneath.
Everything was green, symbolic of the rainforest. They had a trustee building
down the road, so once we got done playing in this ballroom, they took us
to a little bar down on a lower street, then security took us to our trustee
room where we were able to stay the night. It was kind of weird to have their
board meeting room right there, and they showed us to our room that had
bunk beds.

George and Billy were under me and Tommy. After we were there for a while, Tommy yells over from his bunk bed, "Hey Al, Al. Check Billy out." You got to keep in mind, as I said, Billy was "well blessed." So reluctantly I lean over my bunk bed to look down at Billy, and Billy was always naked or damn near. There he is lying there with his package laying off to the right, just about laying over his right hip.

Tommy says, "Hey Roop, look down at Billy. He's signaling for a right-hand turn." And I'll tell you, I just about fell out of my bunk bed laughing my ass off at him.

We rented a big boat from B&B Riverboats in Cincinnati; it took one hundred and ten friends. We took two Greenlawn buses, plus some people drove, and we picked everybody up in Delaware and more at the Ruckmore when we went through Columbus headed for Cincinnati. The owners had a great idea. It was a boat called the "Katiki." They thought we should set up and be playing before they let anyone on board. They also had us set up in the front facing to the back, with waves and the shoreline moving backwards. It felt odd. We went about two hours up the river, then turned back. They treated us wonderful. We were the first band to ever sell them out of beer and liquor. We were the most profitable band they ever had on a four-hour excursion.

Another good one was the Slippery Noodle Inn, in Indianapolis. Probably two of the best blues bars I ever found are the Soup Kitchen in Detroit and the Slippery Noodle in Indy. The Noodle was originally an old hotel; in fact there are pictures and plaques of authenticity that John Dillinger lived there when it was an old hotel. In the back it had a carriage house where he blew the hell out of the brick wall and there is a plaque there. Later they turned

that carriage house into a two-floor bar. The Hayloft was a bar and downstairs was a big bar and stage.

In the front was a great little bar and another bandstand, and up the staircase the first room on the right was John Dillinger's room. It was just amazing. The people who owned it were great people and showed us around. The owner bought some memorabilia from the movie *The Blues Brothers.* He had the American Express check they paid their tab with at Bob's Country Bunker. He also bought Stevie Ray Vaughn's SRV guitar at an auction.

Another night we were there, we were playing in the front room, the smaller room, up in the old hotel part and Jeff Healey, the great blind guitar player, who was in the movie *Roadhouse,* had been playing at the

Vogue Theatre in Indy. When they got done, I suppose about midnight, they came over because the Noodle was open until four a.m., and we were still playing. Jeff Healey was there with his drummer and their bus driver.

Billy said, "Jeff, would you like to play one?"

He said, "Yeah, I would like to play, I don't want to sing, you could unplug the monitor." Jeff came up and sat down, George McDonald, gave him his guitar.

The drummer yelled up to the stage, "Jeff, it's an old Marshall." He turned around to George's amp and started dialing it in and checking out the tone.

Then Billy Simpson yells, "Hey George, leave it where the blind guy set it." We played a few with Jeff, and his drummer ended up coming up and playing.

I forget, we were in the big room, and I remember looking over where you came in and Carrot Top was leaning on the wall, digging the music. I thought that was pretty cool.

We were at Stash & Little Brothers once with a kick-ass blues band, Pappa Chubby. They were on their No Sleep Tour, and had been in Europe, then in New York. Then they came to Stash & Little Brothers right across the street from Dick's Den, Columbus. We opened the show, and boy, he was kind of wild. The leader turned around to the bass player and said, "I told you, you are too fucking loud."

We couldn't believe it, later on we got talking to the bass man, and I said, "Boy how do you do it; he's nuts."

He said, "I just hate that son of a bitch." And they were travelling in a window van with a trailer carrying all of their stuff, wouldn't that be hard?

We were also there with Matt Murphy from the Blues Brothers Band and movie, and I was very happy to meet him and watch him play.

There's a bar in Delaware beside Kintz, called Stop 42. Many probably don't know they have a big backroom bar and stage. Twenty-five years ago we played there with Chicago blues legend Koko Taylor and her band. She was famous for the song "The Wang Dang Doodle, All Night Long."

We also played there with The Lonnie Brooks Band from Chicago a few months later. They got hotel rooms and K.F.C. We were lucky enough to open for them, and have some of their chicken.

Billy was about ready to retire from the Barrel House Band. We had one official night left to go. We were at

Koko Taylor

the VIP on Frantz Road in Dublin. That was a pretty kick-ass place run by my buddy Dean Hughes who I drove the limousines with, and Pat Cashman, my buddy from Buns and Cashman's drive-thru here in Delaware. He had a beautiful custom coach from Custom Coach in Arlington. And for our last night we met in Delaware and rode out to the VIP on Frantz Road. I remember Tommy and me and George cutting fruit for our shots of Cuervo Gold, drinking Budweiser in this big pretty red, chrome and stainless steel bus that looked like Budweiser.

I came back to Delaware with them and got in my car, down around Hills Miller or something. My old Pontiac went straight, the road curved right, and I totaled it in a bean field.

I walked to the house nearby, and the door was opened and the owner said, "I knew you would be here in a minute. I've heard that sound before."

He stuck a Busch beer in my hand. I waited for a ride home in a couple hundred-dollar car, and I said, "Boy, there's a blues song, I went to work in a half-million dollar custom coach and road home in a two hundred dollar taxi. Damn."

***

NOT TOO LONG AFTER that, Billy left the band; my god was he something. But Willie Pooch was filling in. We got a great job to play for the end of the year dock party at Alum Creek State Park Boat Docks. They were doing a big BBQ. We were lucky, the guy that booked the party for us had two forty foot pontoon style houseboats, with big 12X12 patios in the front, a big living room, a kitchen, and bedrooms. George McDonald, the guitar player, me and Willie Pooch stayed for the night. We had fun on the boat after the gig at the dock.

The next morning we were all about ready to leave. Willie puts his suit back on, and I remember plain as day, it was a purple alligator bright purple suit, slacks, sport coat with a white alligator shirt and a purple hat, and purple alligator shoes to match. He was purple from head to toe. It was about eight in the morning, and he was strolling off the patio of the boat, and I tell you, I never laughed so damn hard in my life. George and I; it was killing us.

I wish I had movie of it. This good old boy in his rust-colored Carhatts, was sitting out there with his hoodie up and all of his fishing gear, tackle box and his cooler. He's out there toward the end of the dock near us. And Willie strolls off the boat in this full purple suit from head to toe, and he tips his hat to the guy and says, "Top of the morning to you," and just walks on.

This poor old boy looks over at me and George standing on the front of the boat and he says, "Goddamn, he looks like a lure."

***

WELL, BACK TO MUSIC and the focus of the view from the stage. You know, when you play stuff like "Bad, Bad Leroy Brown" or "Color My World" or "Joy to the World," some of the stuff that you played over and over every night, playing just happens. You end up daydreaming, looking around the room. It gives you time to see who's there, smile at a table, or point your drum stick at a friend, staying in touch. Top forty isn't like playing kick-ass blues or funk, where you really have to get into it, every moment. You just daydream a little bit because the song becomes second nature, you could watch people, bartenders, and bar bosses, all of the dumb shit they do.

When you are looking out there and you see a girl or guy headed to the dance floor, sometimes times they turn around, it looks like their exhaling, blowing air out, backing on to the dance floor. Get down brother.

I liked watching people at one table where they started normal as they drank and the hours passed, you could guess with yourself, which of about three ways this will end up.

Dad always loved bands, also pretty bartenders. He was no dummy. He thought they were pretty cool, but they always have two or three kids.

We laughed about that for years because it was true most of the time, and when I met Karyol, she had a son, Matt. Dad said, "Boy, she is a pretty little girl. That's a cute mommy and son."

I think he was happy for me, and I got to tell him that after his story of they always have three or four kids, I said, "Yeah, and the great thing is, she only has one." I think he got a chuckle out of that. He remembered the story, I got me the bartender, and she only had one, and he's a good one.

***

ANOTHER ED STORY... We had this picture of us at Christmas, Dad, Ed my brother-in-law Phil and myself, we put mom's wigs on, some earrings, and we were all decorated up for Christmas putting on a show. That was kind of our responsibility at Christmas, how silly could we get.

After dad passed, we took mom out a lot. We had her out at Grand Lake St. Mary's. We took a pontoon around the lake to hit all the fun spots. (I found out later that was the home of our buddy Buckeye Boys BBQ Dave).

Then we went back to our hotel, out there. And again, it was me, Ed and Phil, and we were doing some synchronized swimming to show Sister Ginny

Ed, Dad, Me and Phil

and Mom just how much we had our shit together.

Me and Mohney had played the Bill Kates show. We had played through the week and on one Sunday they come to my house, with my buddy Gary Van from Florida.

They were telling me we got to go to Dubois, Pennsylvania, to do a grand re-grand opening of a hotel up there. Bill Kates booked it and was the singer in the band. I said, "No, I'm not going. I feel like shit. I'm not going anywhere." This was early Sunday morning.

Gary knew how to get over me a little bit. He said, "Come on, Mohney and Kates will take the old van with the equipment in it. We got your drums loaded up, and we can take Kate's, the booking agent's Cadillac, it will be fun. When we get up there we will get a steak dinner, and good money, and we get to open this place. This is going to be good shit." So he talked me into it. It was probably about eleven a.m.

So we take off and in the Cadillac. Somewhere around Akron we found a place where we could get a bottle of wine. We had the Caddy, a soul station on the radio, a bottle of wine, and we were following the equipment truck, and slapping hands.

It turned out it was a hell of a night. We did the grand opening, and just so we wouldn't get screwed out of our steaks on the first break. We took our steaks because by the end of the night they always go, "Oh, what a shame. We are out of them." We crammed it all in and got back to town. We probably got home at six in the morning.

***

WHO WAS MY FAVORITE BLUES GUY?

Well, it's Albert Collins, Johnny Guitar Watson, Buddy Guy and Doctor John.

Where is the best blues bar?

There are so many that are incredible, but the best blues bar I have ever been to in my life was the Soup Kitchen in Detroit. It's gone now. Everybody in the world played there, and all of their pictures were around the walls. In the day it was called the Soup Kitchen because in World War II it was open twenty-four hours a day and for twenty-five cents you could get a grilled cheese and a cup of soup. The Soup Kitchen was cool. Probably one of the best blues bar in the world. Now it is Buddy Guy's on Wabash in Chicago.

***

WE WERE TALKING ABOUT playing places that are kind of weird. We worked on the riverboat, and going down the river, you could see out of your peripheral vision the bank going up and down on the left and right. You could kind of get used to it.

One of the worst was in theatres like the Newport or the Palace. In places like that the stage light guys are doing lights, and you are playing music. You might be playing in 4/4 time, 1, 2, 3, 4, you're playing that. And the light guy might be doing the lights faster or slower. That kind of screws you up worse than a really bad dancer.

Playing outside always sucks. That's why nobody likes to play private parties. If you are playing a party, and you are behind the singers and guitar players as a drummer, you can't hear shit. You just play along with whatever guitar you can hear, and you don't hear any vocals at all. Sometimes in big theatres you hear the vocals a second after they are sang; they bounce back at you, which is kind of weird.

If any of us had our choice, none of us like to play outside. It's always hot, and it sounds like shit. You don't feel like you are playing with the rest of the band.

Or it's a big place indoor place where the sound bounces back off of you.

In a big place the coolest thing in the world is when you hit the bass pedal and you hear it rocket through the room, that big concussion. Boom, boom. There's really nothing like it. It helps you play simple because you can hear the bass, every beat so well, you can hear your snare drum crack and you don't add anything unneeded. You just lay it in the pocket.

*****

WE PLAYED AT THE Women's Correctional Institute in Marysville. My buddy Mark Kreis had Apollo Recording Studio in Marysville and a great band. He had me, Don Beck and Willie Pooch play at the correctional institute. They checked us out quite well going in.

I somehow remember they checked the van out underneath it with mirrors, we took our belts off because you couldn't have those. We were to play out on the ball field. I think there were three colors of shirts the gals wore for security levels; they had green, hot pink, and whatever. Pooch was walking across the property over to the ball diamond where we were going to play, and he's got a hot pink shirt on, that was the maximum security color shirt of the prison. The bad girls and Pooch.

*****

ANOTHER GREAT CONCERT with Pooch was one I was surprised to be invited in on. It was at The Faucet Center at OSU on Olentangy River Road, the Ohio State University Faucet Center. They had an old time radio program for Christmas. It was hosted by Phil Dirt and the Dozers and other special guests like Dave Powers. Pooch got invited, and he wanted me to be the drummer. We met at the Ruckmore early in the morning; I think we had to be at the Faucet Center around seven in the morning.

Phil Dirt and the Dozers were just kicking ass. And it came our turn; I think around eight a.m., the Dozers with Powers playing keyboards and us. Playing one of my very favorite Christmas songs ever, I forget who did it originally, but the Eagles did a version of "I'll Be Home for Christmas." with the lyrics "Bells will be ringing/that sad, sad song." It was just beautiful. And we had this huge orchestra playing with us. Man, I had goose bumps, one of my greatest Christmas moments ever.

The Faucet Center stage was covered across the front of it with hundreds and hundreds of red flowers, with a great crowd, and it was going out live on the radio.

***

SOMEHOW THAT MADE ME think about another Ed story. We took the family and our little 82-year old mom to Lake Chautauqua, New York, about four hours northeast of us. A pretty damn big lake, it used to be connected to Lake Erie. Lucille Ball had a house there, so did the Fords, Dodges and Packards, because it was between Detroit and New York. The town is called Bemus Point.

One day we rented a twenty-four-foot speedboat. We wanted to come down midway in the lake to the Summer Bar; they called it. It was up on a hill like a plantation with rolling grounds coming down to the water. The dock must have been out fifty feet because it was shallow and rocky, and it was pretty choppy water. It was exceptionally choppy this day. We got the boat docked at the end of it, and we went inside and had some drinks with my sister and

my brother-in-law, Ed, my wife, some other friends, and Mom. We thought, well we better get this boat back; it's not getting any better. We would take the boat back and come back in the van.

We went down to get into the boat, and Ed had it running. Ed was a good boatman. There was a "T" out at the end of the dock, out about fifty feet off the shore. Ed throws the bow rope, throws it in reverse right away, hits the throttle, quickly to back out. The bow rope had a knot in it that caught right between the boards on that hunk of shit dock. We were backing out with the nose dipping down in the water backing out pretty fast, the rope snags the dock and pulls part off. Ed shuts the boat down because we knew we had a problem, and slowly the whole dock leans to the left and goes into the water. My sister is laughing so hard she

pees her pants. My wife is laughing with all of us. You had to laugh because this hunk of shit dock just disappeared.

We looked over at this boat coming in and this lady was standing toward the front with a rope in her hand ready to tie it off, but there wasn't anything there, there wasn't shit left.

We had about thirty minutes to get the boat back, and then drive back to the bar. We got back and the caretaker of the property was on a big John Deere cutting grass. We pull in in the van and go in to see how Mom, Phil and the gang is doing. This guy is tucking his shirt in and walking up to us.

He said, "Well, do you have something to tell me?"

Ed said, "Yeah, we fucked your dock up. We're sorry."

He said, "Well, you didn't have to be laughing about it."

Ed said, "Yeah, I threw the rope; the rope caught the dock, and it pulled the dock down. My sister laughed and peed her pants. Al's wife just about peed her pants. We're sorry but it was funny, and we had to go because there wasn't anything to tie up to."

He gave us hell, and Ed said, "Well, we left our poor little mom here for collateral."

And as it turned out the people inside said, "Oh, screw him. That dock was in bad shape, and it needed replaced." I think they bought us a round of drinks. But anyhow, that was the end of the dock at the Summer Bar at Lake Chautauqua.

***

ANOTHER GREAT ONE WAS with my buddy Tom Backus, T-Bone. He was putting a band together called T-Bone and the Usual Suspects with Willie Pooch, Donnie Hobbs from Detroit, T-Bone, myself, and his brother, Cheeseburger, Dave Backus. We were going to do a live recording at Dick's Den on High Street. My brother bartended there during the day for eighteen years or so. We

T-BONE and the USUAL SUSPECTS *featuring Willie Pooch*

Jake & Elwood
Wilson Pickett

LONG LIVE THE BLUES
Memories and Imagination

Albert Collins
Stevie Ray Vaughan

went down to do the live album, and while the recording guy was setting up,

we went over to the Blue Danube, ate; and went back and did the album, T-Bone and the Usual Suspects featuring Willie Pooch. It was one of the best nights Dick's Den ever had. That was a fun one. It was fun doing it, in the studio, and the release party. T-Bone did a hell of a good job. This group of guys he put together weren't done yet, we'll be back.

T-Bone Rounded up the Usual Suspects Dec. 3rd 1994

"T-Bone and the Usual Suspects" featuring Willie Pooch, was rounded up for a one night live recording. To their surprise it resulted in recognition around the world.

Brothers Tom "T-Bone" and Dave Backus (guitar and Hammond B-3) asked Al Roop to play drums along with bass guitarist Donnie Hopps who drove down from Detroit. Then they asked the great Willie Pooch to do vocals. The band had never been together to perform, live unrehearsed fun blues was the theme for the evening, by the third tune when Pooch took the stage the magic had begun.

Since the recording "Live at Dick's Den" the band has been doing several shows a month. One of the shows was with the Jeff Beck and Santana Show at the Polaris Amphitheater in 1995. They have been reviewed by blues publications and radio stations not only in the USA but also in Germany, Italy, Holland and Japan. Like T-Bone said, "The blues gods must have been looking down on us."

Special thanks to Dave Tyack, Billy Simpson, and Tony Stidam for filling in at times or what would we have done?

Great Sunday afternoon Blues treats.

Kate's Sherry Cake
1/2 cup Pecans, chopped
1 pkg Duncan Hines butter
reci
1 pkg
Grease an
pans. Place
Pour batte
Remove fr
Hot Sherry
1 cup
1 stick
Place ingr
sauce. 20

1/2 cup DRINKING Sherry
1/2 cup Water

Dick's Den Gang

If you get near one of these towns,
stop by their number one blues club:

Pittsburgh, PA . . . Blues Cafe . . . . Carson Street at 19th
Cleveland, OH . . . Wilbert's . . . . West 9th by the Flats
Detroit, MI . . . . . . Soup Kitchen . . . . In the Rivertown District
Indianapolis, IN . . Slippery Noodle Inn . . . South & Meridian
Chicago, IL. . . . . . House of Blues . . . . Marina City Towers

All have excellent food

Recording and Mix Engineer
Jay Kuehn from
Harmonic Park Creative Group,
Detroit, MI (313) 965-4343

Produced by Lionheart
For band information write
P.O. Box 632
Westerville, OH 43089

Woodshed Records Inc.
www.woodshedrecords.com
P.O. Box 510672
Livonia, MI 48151
Please contact us for CD sales or schedule

Our thanks to:
Drivers, Ron Schaib and Phil White, Jay Kuehn and Brent Patrick, also Big Chris and John Crabtree, T-Shirt, Poster, etc. Art and Design by Todd Wernicke (614) 486-9075, e-mail: Todd@beai.net., Insert Design by Roy Prond, Rich Cosmo for 1000 Hotwings for the road, QFMs Wags & Elliott for moral support, Cruisin Tunes, Tim Reed at Prime Time Recording Studio, Sherly King, Mom and Pop Hopps in Detroit, also Nan, Ed and the gang at Dick's, Everyone at Custom Coach Corp. (614) 481-8881.

***

SOMEWHERE AROUND THE LATE nineties at Buckeye Lake, we were scheduled to play at the Port Bar, the best bar at Buckeye Lake. Some of our best friends ran the place, Sue, Mark, and Mike. I was supposed to be there with the Barrel House Band, but we didn't do that job. We ended up doing a flood relief party at the Bogey Inn with six other bands for disaster relief. I think it was a screw up in my booking.

It was ten years later; we were coming back from Pittsburgh, and we went to the Port Bar on a Sunday. I remembered the date because we were supposed to be there on August 7, which was my father's birthday, ten years earlier. Anyhow, we told Mark we were going to play. He said, "Oh, I don't have the time to advertise or anything. I don't have the money."

We said, "Well, it doesn't matter. We're here, and we want to play for you." And we didn't know what Mark had. He went back and found one of our flyers; he had the flyer for August 7 ten years earlier.

Introducing the band he said, "Can you believe this? I have some dumbass buddies who have showed up an hour late to meet me for a drink, or two days late to fix a cooler, even a week late. I've had friends do a lot of things, but nobody is a bigger dumbass than Roop, who shows up ten years late, to the day. I have the flyer to prove it." And he did.

. We were playing, and it came time for T-Bone's solo, the Port has an outside barbecue bar and had a separate bandstand over by the water. We could hear T-Bone playing, kicking ass like Stevie Ray. We look out in the bay near the stage, T-Bone was standing on the bow of a speedboat, just cranking. They did circles out in the bay, and we were playing over on the stage.

Go to the Port and have some BBQ, and tell them some dumbass sent you.

***

ME AND POOCH WERE in a hotel room in Athens, it was quite a moment and Willie said, "Al, we got to go on the road one more time before we're too damn old. Let's put a good tour together." We sat there in bed and ate our hot dogs and sipped Willie's gin. "Maybe we can hit some great spots and really make it a good album."

And one thing led to another, and the idea turned into what we called *Five Nights, Five States, and Five Blues Bars*. Consecutive nights then come back to town and play at the El Dorado on the sixth night. We worked on it and worked on it. Columbus Custom Coach gave us a bus, but we had to pay for the driver.

We booked the bars: Monday, the Blue Note, in Pittsburgh at 19th and Carson; Cleveland, Wilbert's Blues Bar downtown; Detroit's Soup Kitchen, one of the greatest; Indianapolis, the Slippery Noodle Inn; and then we ended up at the Chicago House of Blues. And, boy that was great. Shirley King was there, B.B.'s daughter, and she sang with us that night.

Willie's idea of doing one more tour and recording was great. We did it with the guys from the Dick's Den album.

The bass player from Detroit had a buddy with a recording studio. He went on the bus with his recording equipment. I took my brother-in-law, Phil, and another friend, Brent Patrick, for a tee shirt guy. We loaded up the bus, put our signs on the side that said *"5 Nights on the Road with Blues Man Willie Pooch; 5 Nights, 5 States, 5 Blues Clubs"* and hit the road. We went to Cosmo's in Dublin because he said if we went there he would start us out with one hundred chicken wings to get to Pittsburgh. We did that at about noon. We rolled into Pittsburgh and did the gig, and rumbled through the night with the ol' bus shaking and rumbling, eating chicken wings and having a shot and talking about the first night. We wanted to be in a different town each night, and we played on the bus like our idols did for years, like B.B. King did.

The next day we were in Cleveland on the east side of the Flats area, getting ready to play at Wilbert's. That was a wonderful day, and a lot of friends showed up.

The next day we made it to the Soup Kitchen in Detroit right on the river in old town where hundreds and hundreds of bands had played. They had all of their pictures of the blues and jazz era filling the walls, the red drapes

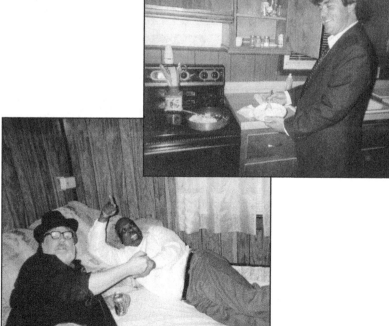

behind the bandstand. We were playing where everybody that was anybody had played. It was a great old wood blues bar. We looked out the door, and there was T-Bone playing to a cab driver, putting on his show.

On our way to Indy we stopped at the Auburn Cord Duesenberg Museum where they made Auburns and Cords, and all kinds of cool cars were there. It was Auburn, Indiana. It turns out the museum was closed, but the curator was there and he saw the big old tour bus; and he said, "Well, for you guys, you can do anything you want. Come on in."

Willy says, "Hey, can I go out to the bus and make me a taste, a little vodka?"

And he said, "You can do anything you want."

We saw celebrities' Duesenbergs and Cords, even the design and tooling rooms; then we made our way to Indy.

The next day we made our way to Chicago, which was the best. We stayed in Merrillville, Indiana; and we met these poor gals who were at the desk, we said, "Why don't you come up to Chicago and see us play? We will get you in." I think my brother-in-law said that.

She said, "Oh darling, we don't drive no highways." She asked if they could get on the bus with us. We took a little nap, and I remember the hotel door opened. I was staying in Brett's room, and I could hear the bus running, and that meant it's time to brush your teeth and get on the road to Chicago.

I was brushing my teeth and Brett said, "Al, you might want to look out here."

I remember looking in the mirror brushing my teeth, and I saw a big gal with grey, kind of frizzy hair, God bless her, in a pink leisure suit with a pink

purse. I walked out, and she said, "Oh, I sure hope you weren't lying to me. Me and my niece want to go to Chicago with you." They were just the nicest people, and we took them on in with us. We got to Chicago, and there's the girls stepping out of Mercedes with hose with the seam in the back and high heels, all decked out. We were with the girls from Merrillville, Indiana, and we got them a front row seat.

And, by God, they just had a ball. And to our surprise, Shirley King, B.B. King's daughter, had opened the evening, and she sat in with us that night; and we were having a ball. She called herself the daughter of the blues. We played to three a.m. in the there. The boss said sometimes it dies off early there, but it never died off; and they were still paying the cover to get in there at two in the morning.

He said, "Boy, I wish you were going to be around for awhile." Shirley ended up singing "Hoochie, Coochie Woman" with us. She was singing, "I'm 36 in the chest, 24 in the waist," and I was thinking, "Boy, I'm not buying that." I was right behind her. Shirley's a big gal, then she said, "I'm 58 in the hips and a whole lot more." The place went crazy; it was a song we kept on the album.

All those tapes that were recorded at the House of Blues had to be sent to California to their home office to be cleared for quality that represented the House of Blues. It took about two months to get them back, so we could start doing the studio work on the album; and, by God, it's got Shirley King doing, "I'm 36, 24, 58 and a whole lot more." It was just great.

Coming back into town the next day off I70, we came up High Street because we were going to do a coming home party at the El Dorado at Morse and High. They had kicked in on the album.

Coming past Dick's Den where my brother worked, we had called him and told him we were coming through, and we were probably only going about ten miles an hour in the coach. There were about thirty of them outside, standing out there for us, saluting us driving by. That made the five nights on the road ending very special. It was good to see my brother, Jimmy, Nan who owned Dick's and the gang there.

Another funny thing that happened on the tour, one of my best friends, Timmy Sullivan, who helped me rebuild Roop Brothers Bar, Ol' Timmy showed up at four of the five bars on the tour. To my surprise, in Indy he showed up dressed like a Blues Brother, with black suit, white shirt, black hat, and black sunglasses. I was dying laughing behind my drums. I look one way I see Timmy, and the other way I see Carrot Top.

They put us up in a house right down the road, a couple of blocks away. The house had pool tables and a downstairs. The living room was all beds. Well, me and Timmy looked around for something to eat. I'm sure we had a bottle of Jager. The bar didn't close until four in the morning, and then we went to this house.

We found one stick of butter, salt and pepper shakers and a box of Uncle Ben's rice. We put that in a cast iron skillet with a whole stick of butter and our Jager.

Timmy went to Chicago also, and the main drink we were doing there was lemon drops. It was pretty cool because the House of Blues is in Marina City, the Twin Towers, the two round buildings, on the near north side. There is a valet parking circle off to the side.

We sat on the cement wall and watched the boats coming up and down the Chicago River between the near north side and the loop, the downtown Chicago. Looking in front of us we could see the bottom half of the Sears Tower, then there were clouds; and then we could see the top of the Sears Tower.

Along comes a gal from inside the club, and she said, "I've been looking all over for you." She had a tray of lemon drops. She said, "This is the last of them. We don't have anymore lemon vodka, so I am glad I found you guys." She came clear out there in the valet parking. We had our lemon drops, and it was probably Timmy who toasted, "That's to Crabby," a good friend that sponsored part of the tour, John Crabtree. Another one of our buddies who helped us was Yogi who ran the Ruck.

***

What kind of kit do I play, what set of drums do I use? I've always used Ludwig. When I was real young, I had a black pearl set of some kind, and they weren't too good. But once I really started playing, I got a set of Ludwig Vista Lights. When they originally came out, they were the very first ones to be clear, plastic drums, kind of a piece shit in a way. They came apart in

Drums before I outfitted them and after

the seams and a lot of people had problems with them breaking, but they were just so damn pretty and different. I had blue clear drums, and I got them in 1968.

I play a typical five-piece set, that's a snare drum between legs, the bass drum, a floor tom and two side mounted toms above the bass, with two crash cymbals, a small one on my left and a larger one on my right, with a little deeper tone. I used a twenty-four inch ride on my left, which is backwards.

I'm right handed, but played left handed up top; that's just how I taught myself. A little trick I used was if I got a new cymbal, and it sounded too bright or rang too long, I would put a small piece of duct tape under it to get the right tone. I've always used a Ludwig speed king pedal. I never upgraded to the ones that sit higher off the ground and chain drive or whatever. I like the old, regular, low-profile speed king. I even have a back up my buddy Roger Maze, another drummer, gave me.

I got a letter in response to something I had written, I guess from Bill Ludwig, the owner of Ludwig Drums; so I will share that with you.

Later on I moved to a better set of Ludwigs and retired the Vista Lights. I found a set of solid five-ply maple Ludwig drums. I got them used at Big Daddy's Music Store in Delaware. The same size kit, two side mounts, four tom bass and snare. Smokey Robinson's drummer had told me, take the vinyl off of them, the white pearl, and just leave the natural wood. He had a stain on his. He said just keet them oiled nicely, and boy they sounded great.

The pretty sparkly coverings that they put on them or the white pearl like these were, were plastic and he said, "Get rid of that, and let them breathe like a fine guitar or a fine violin. The tone is much richer and better without that shit on them." He also said, "Now don't screw them up like everybody does. They're wood, and with the crummy coverings are gone, that's so beautiful."

I said, "I should urethane them and really make them pretty."

He said, "By using that shit you are putting the plastic back on them. Once you take that plastic layer off and get down to the wood drum, you definitely don't want to urethane them." He told me in detail about that; and he also

Ludwig & Musser Percussion Instruments and Accessories

Feb. 15, 1991

Mr. Al Reep (?) Roop
2743 E. Powell Road
Westerville, Ohio 43081

Dear Al:

Thank you for your wonderful letter and the terrific
promotional material enclosed with it! Seldom if ever
has anyone gone to such great lengths as you have to portray
21 years of traveling with a Ludwig vistalite set! Many,
many thanks to you my friend for thinking of doing this and
especially for the many compliments expressed within your
letter.

Please pardon the informality of my greeting. Although we have
never met I feel I know you from somewhere. Also, try as I
might I just could'nt make out your name when you signed your
letter to me. I hope you don't mind!

I am glad you like the blue vistalite drums---one of my con-
coctions of many years ago. You must take very, very good care
of them. Many did not and we had substantial return due to
cracking and lap separations and the like that when the price of
oil shot up in 1974 due to the Arab embargo, we finally, and
most regretfully terminating all production of the vistalite
line.

This Vistalite era was indeed a colorful era for my company.
Living in my memory always will be the sight of all the many
colors linedup in the assembly department ready for packing---
all colors of the rainbow and then some! Stripes, spirals,
checkerboards----just about every design youcould immagine!

Anyway, its all gone now and forever. That is why I especially
like your remembrance of days of glory now past. Again, many
thanks for your wonderful, wonderful compliments!

Sincerely yours,

Wm. F. Ludwig Jr.
Consultant

William F. Ludwig Jr.
1080 Nerge Rd. • Suite 106 • Elk Grove, IL 60007
(708) 307-8866

said, "Go ahead and get these mounting rings."

Typically the two side-mounted toms above the bass drum are on a post
that goes into the top center of the bass drum, and it's like a bracket tree that
holds the side-mounted toms. The problem is the drums are heavy, and those
two tom toms are pushing down on the center of the top of the bass drum,

and it could restrict tone, the quality of the tone. So you mount these rings that go half-way around the drum, instead of the side-mounted toms hanging from one point with all of their weight hanging, one to the left and one to the right on that tree above the bass drum, these rubber-mounted brackets that go half way around each of the drums mount to the cymbal stands so the cymbal stand is holding the bracket; and the bracket is holding the drum, and it's not hanging so the tone is better on all of drums.

That's what I've been playing with for a hell of a long time. I upgraded my stool. We were playing at a bar down near Worthington, on Wilson-Ridge Road, and my seat broke. I had seen a great seat in the Blues Brothers' movie that was just a round cooler, and I thought I would check that out.

Instead of one hundred fifty bucks for another drummer's throne seat, I went down to the Worthington Hardware store, and sure enough they had some nice round coolers, just the right height to sit on. I took the vinyl padded part off my old seat and just dry-walled screwed it through the lid up through the cooler so it had the padded top. It worked out great. I keep my bass pedal, extra sticks, and oil for the bass pedal in it. I can keep everything in there, and it is easy to carry into the gig, set my drums up, take the lid off my seat, and there is all my stuff.

Hell, it was only fifty bucks instead of one hundred fifty, and it works better, and when we play outside jobs, I would take my supplies out of my seat and load it with ice and cold beer.

The other thing I did that some people thought was pretty screwy was I never messed with cases. Most drummers folded up and telescoped the legs of the cymbal stands. I didn't even collapse them; I left them in the heights I played them.

I had a rug and, in fact, you can even buy them. They are called a "gig" rug, to set your stuff up on. They are four foot by five or six. I bought a rug at Wal-Mart or something. I put all of my cymbal stands on it and roll ed them up. You grab the roll and put it in the car. It worked great because sometimes you worked bars or patios that were cement or a wood, with no rug your set will walk away from you, and you have to keep pulling back the bass drum and pulling it back. The cymbal stands can move too.

There has been many times when I didn't have a rug, I would go outside a bar or restaurant, and I would see if they had the usual mat or rug that drops off for their entrance, and well, I would borrow it.

My patented (as I called it) gig rug hardware case, cool drums like Smokey Robinson's drummer had, and my multi-purpose stool like the guy in the Blues Brothers, was perfect.

***

WHAT MUSIC STORES DID we go to? Well in the early days, everybody liked Whitey Lunzar's. I used to run into great musicians there, like Budd Fowler, George Mobley, and Mark Chatfield. Chatfield has done real well for himself. He's got Cowtown Guitars in Vegas now. Occasionally, I watch Pawn Stars, and they always call Cowtown Guitars. The other one was Coil on High Street down around Clintonville. I always bought my cymbals at Uncle Sam's Pawn Shop at Fourth and Main. There was no reason to pay near four hundred bucks for a nice cymbal at a music store when you could go down there and get one like new for one hundred fifty bucks. Of course, Roger Maze's Music Barn in Delaware was a good one, and Greg Houston, Big Daddy, had Big Daddy's Family Music.

Speaking of Chatfield, I used to go to this little bar on Worthington Road. It's called the Worthington Café. Now it's Donaricks. We were sitting in there one day, and Chatfield lived up the road. He left and came back in and said, "Oh hell, I'll have another one with you. I guess I'm not going anywhere." He must have pissed his girlfriend off or something. He was driving a Bronco, and he went out all four tires were flat.

Later on in Delaware, Crossroads Music Store was an awfully good one. They have been gone for a couple of years. I still fill in playing when needed for somebody. I like to play festivals where there are five or six bands, and the drums are already set up, and you only play forty-five minutes. I miss Crossroads for when I need sticks. A really cool thing that happened at Crossroads involved Eric Clapton who has a place not too far south of Delaware. Eric is married to a local girl. Everybody wonders if we had any sightings, and he showed up once at the Brown Jug Restaurant. Eric and a buddy of his sat on the patio and had a nice quiet afternoon.

They then went across the street to Crossroads. A buddy of mine, Timmy, was working. Tim is a real soft-spoken nice guy with real long hair and a long beard, sometimes braided with beads in it. He said, "Shit Roop, you wouldn't believe it. Clapton came in. I know it was Clapton. I knew instantly who it was. I was so dumbfounded all I could do was stare. He came walking up toward me, and I'm' still freaking out. He sticks his hand out to shake and says, 'Eric.'"

The new music store in town is owned and operated by some of the teachers and band members from Crossroads. It's called The Delaware Music Academy, with the best including Adam Furay, Jayson Brechtel and Gaetano Nicolose. My buddy Adam Vaughn, who has been helping me with this book, also played in bands with some of those guys.

***

I REMEMBER AN OCCASION, it was pretty unusual for the Pooch Band, Andy Robinson, "Robo" and of course, Yorkie Proctor, Rick Calura and I were at the Lakes Country Club to do a short party. We set up, and I'm just hanging out. I'm kind of wondering where everybody is when it is getting closer to playing time. I see Willie over at the buffet, loading up a plate and I asked where Yorkie was.

He said, "Well, he went out to his van and got his putter; he is out putting on the ninth green right there, near the patio where we were playing." There was my buddy out there in his shorts and his flowered shirt and his Converse tennis shoes, and just enjoying putting on the gorgeous ninth green at the Lakes Country Club.

Pooch was eating, and then to make it better, I hear Big Robo, "Hey Roop," from across the room, "You are not going to believe this. No fucking Jager." So we played a little bit, and I had this stupid idea, right down the road is the Ruckmore. They don't normally have a band, but I've done a couple of things there. I called the manager Yogi, who is usually game for anything. I said, "Andy's flipping. We are doing this great job, but they don't have any Jager."

He said, "Well, what do you want to do?"

I said, "Do you think you could throw them a little money, and we will come down and play a couple of hours for you?"

He started moving tables and chairs out of the way and said, "A couple of hundred bucks, and all the Jager you want." We finished the last song and backed the truck up and started putting equipment in. I didn't even take the cymbals off the stands.

We packed everything up and Rick Calura said, "We haven't done anything fun like just crashing another bar for the hell of it for over ten years."

So we get down there, and we are set up and ready to play within a few minutes. Of course, Andy said, "First things first. Let's take care of business, Roop." He had little beer glasses, and a couple of those popped up for me and Andy, full to the brim. We finished the first song, and there is Yogi and that big ass smile on his face. Everybody had more beers and glasses of Jager, and we just had a hell of a good time. We sure thanked the Ruck and Yogi for letting some guys have some fun and do something on the spur of the moment. That's the shit; that is what life is all about.

***

DRUMMER JOKES, you know there must be a hundred of them out there.

Here's one of them, How do you know when the drum riser's level? The drool runs out of both sides of his mouth.

Or, what's the difference between a mutual fund and a drummer? A mutual fund will eventually mature and be worth something.

Or, how do you know when a drummer is knocking on your door? The knock speeds up.

Why did the drummer cross the road? His dick was stuck in the chicken.

Or one of my favorites: What's the difference between a drummer and a pizza? A pizza can feed a family of four.

My favorite musician joke, not drummer related is this guy does a scratch-off, and wins a million bucks. He is so happy, and they're all having a beer and he says, "Geez, a poor old guitar player like me."

His buddy says, "Well, what are you going to do now that you got a million bucks?"

He says, "Hell, I guess I'll keep going to the gig until the money runs out."

***

ROOP BROTHERS CELEBRATIONS

Real important in my life was the good times and the opportunity to take care of a hell of a lot of friends. We did Roop Brothers Backyard Parties for twenty-nine years. We started it when I realized I had some great friends with the Studio 5 gang, the bar staff and everyone that worked there and the owner, Phil Traxler, and the bands that I had met along the way, including Donnie Beck from Amber Hue, Dave Buzzard from Caliopi, and buddies that ended up life-long friends like Mike Flore and Bob Mohney.

I was living at home, and the folks had a big backyard, but we had to do it on Sundays when we were all off of work. It started being a party for bartenders, servers, musicians and club owners. That's who we dedicated it to.

I told Mom and Dad, I have some good guys coming over like Roger Hunt that I had been playing with at HoJos, and they liked him real well, and they were glad I was playing music for a living. They thought well, that's great; he is going to have a backyard party. Mom and Dad were good hosts. They certainly had musicians visit over the years and had fun with them.

This was 1974 and people started showing up and sitting on blankets out in the yard. We set up an organ, drums and a PA system. They kept coming, and they kept coming. Mom kept pulling out frozen trays of meatballs and different stuff, just in the event that somebody would stop by, and she would need to get into the back-up freezer and get out some goodies. She just kept pulling out tray after tray. God bless her, the little hostess she was.

Roop's 1st Backyard Party 1974
Bill Person, Chuz, Al, Flore, Don Beck, Dave Ellis and Dave Buzzard

Dad was smiling from ear to ear, all of these boys having a beer and tequila in the backyard, and the music, the horn players, even some of my parents friends showed up including Chuz who brought his sax. It turned out to be about one hundred people, and not the twenty we expected, and everyone sat around and enjoyed the great music. All of the guys played. This went on and on and the parties got a little bigger and better as years went by. I eventually built a house with a large backyard and continued with the annual event.

By then, Ed and I were having some shirts made and having fun with that,

Dave Powers, Roger Mayer, Donnie Wilson, Chuck Moore, Flip Jackson, S... terman B... Bostwick and Dan Axt

selling shirts and using the Budweiser Trailer and Budweiser Keg Truck. Then we started bringing in a couple of hay wagons, and putting them beside each other to make a pretty good stage. In the morning we would construct a roof over it and wrap it with Budweiser banners and a killer PA system.

We put the Bud Trailer across in the yard so you could all sit in between them, and had a bonfire for later in the evening. It just couldn't have been better.

It just got bigger and bigger, and I would say, the last ten years we did it; there would be three hundred fifty to four hundred people and easily sixty to seventy musicians.

These were musicians you couldn't buy; they just wanted to come up and be a part of Roop's Celebration. My buddies at Budweiser, I thank Bob North from Del-

Mahoney, Don Beck, Dave Anderson, Dave Vansuch, Al, Scott Strap, Mark Fry of Phil Dirt

Dave Powers, Billy Simpson, Darrell Smith, Bill Bostwick

mar Distributing for being such a good friend for years, and they couldn't hardly believe it either, because we would go through sixteen, seventeen, eighteen kegs at one of these parties. We had guys like Dave Powers and Flip Jackson, Dan Axt, of course T-Bone and Cheeseburger from the Usual Suspects, and Flashback, Rolando and the Velvet King Snakes, Jimmy McGhee, Rusty Bryant, Chuz Alfred, Dirty Billy, the Majestics, Big Al and the Capital City Players, the Ravens, Jim Colbi, Bill Bostwick, Chuck Moore, Scott Strap, Mark Frey, Jed Flahive,, Don Beck, Debra Randell, Harold Smith, Roger Mays, Tom Caple, Dave Lyons, Donnie Wilson, Jimmy Harris, 976 Blues, and Sole Finger all showed up. Incredible, incredible stuff.

We got a couple of good videos out of it. One video was probably one of the last times I got to see Pooch playing old school kick-ass guitar before his arthritis got too bad. But these guys were just amazing.

Big Al Eichenluab & Bob Coker

One year we decided to do it inside, because I had a chance to get the Valleydale Ballroom. The owner were friends of mine, and they knew that

Rusty Bryant & Harold Smith

it was a good crowd that we would bring. I could use the place and they would get the beer sales. And again, we had a great, great line-up. Then to our surprise, I don't know how he had heard about it, Chuz and his great jazz band were playing. Georgie James, an original member of the great Louie Armstrong Band shows up with his wife. He was eighty-six years old at the time, and she was eighty-four and beautiful. She helped Georgie up to the stage and Chuz got a stool for him. She said, "That sonofabitch can't walk too good, but he can sure blow the hell out of that horn." And he did. He and Chuz had the perfect band with his horns and Don Beck playing guitar. Everything was in place for this special celebrity. He did a version of "Over the Rainbow." Everybody, young, old, Jimmy Buffet looking, Harley tee-shirts showing, partiers, just every walk of life, everybody loved seeing this old boy.

He leaned over to the Mic and said, "I'd like to do a song I taught Errol Garner how to play. I call it 'Misty.'" And he played Errol Garner's fabulous "Misty." Again, the place went wild.

At another fun one in the back yard, Fred Pope of Pope Amusement, who did a lot of the midway stuff at the Ohio State Fair, came in one day and saw my buddy Jim Skillman had his big t-shirt trailer.

Detroit Donny, bluesman Bill Buckerfield & Willie Pooch

Dave Lions, Dan Axt, Scott Bock, Pooch & Bill Bostwick

Freddy Pope sees that, so he says, "I'll be back. I'll be right back." He goes to the Ohio State Fair and hitches up his sausage, onion and pepper trailer and just pulls it out of the damn fair, out through the crowd. He decided that he would rather have that trailer in my backyard by the t-shirt trailer and the big beer truck. So here he comes, and we had a beautiful "carney row" there.

Some things you just don't see every day like a regular from Dick's Den, a pretty colorful guy named Andy Vories. He is interesting; he has lived in

Pooch, Mark Cornielius & Mohney

undesirable areas of New York and Cincinnati just to live with other people in different walks of life, and his son did some movies for "Tales From the Crypt." One of them was called "Demenites." Andy just walked around the backyard and talked about his friend Spike Lee and just babbled on. We were filming this one, and we got a good one of it. People got bored listening to his shit about Spike Lee, and when they walked away, he would say, "You will just be back." Later on

Pooch & Jerry Ambrosini

the same people would see him there, drinking his beer, he would say, "See, I told you, you would be back." He would just pick up right where he left off about Spike Lee, goofy shit.

When the camera was on him again, me and Ed go see what they are talking about now; Andy's talking to this couple who are being interviewed, and the girl is grabbing the microphone from the recording guy, and she's going, "Oh, I love microphones, I love them, ah, ah."

And she put her mouth over the microphone, while her boyfriend was pulling her away saying, "Come on now, that's enough of that."

Andy said, "Boy, you could charge admission to this; that was one of the

Flashback Guys - Mohney & Beck

Cold Bud - Just ask Dave

most terrible interviews I ever heard. The boy-friend was trying to pull her away, saying that's enough of that blow job rap, Come on, Honey, we got to go home."

The next thing I see Andy in the backyard, he's talking to a couple of gals he said, "I was just over taking a piss in the neighbor's yard." Eddie said it was fine, that they were out of town. He said, "Then here comes the family out of the house with their daugh-ters home from Welles-ley with a pitcher of ice tea, and I'm pissing in their yard, trying to get

Barrel House Band

it back in my pants." So he's talking to these girls, and he noticed they were looking down at his crotch. His khaki shorts were soaked where he didn't get shut off. He looked at what they were looking at. He just looked at them and said, "Don't you sometimes pee your pants just for fun? I do. I like it." And he just rambles on and on, and on. But Andy was always a lot of fun at the parties and a true legend at Dick's Den too. The guys from the OSU film department got an "A" on the Roop film.

Tarheel Rick Long

Pooch, Dave Anderson and Big Al Eichenlaub

We would take Mom on the town. She was in her eighties, and people used to always say to my Mom when they would see her checking out the band or out with me and Ed. They would say, "Katie, how do you do it?"

She would always replied, "Well, I never have a drink before noon. Only beer." And she was right. She would have a beer in the morning with her scrambled eggs. It always helped her asthma a little bit; and if the asthma got bad at noon, she would switch to a highball, a seven and seven.

***

Improving with age

George James is still jamming

By ROGER MAYES
Delaware THISWEEK

The stage was set. The equipment was on and ready to go. The drums, pianos and guitars were all tuned. The lights came on and the fun part was ready to begin ... the actual playing.

The Roop Brother's Annual Party had begun. This year, the bash was held at the Valley Dale Ballroom in Columbus.

We were all backstage, excited about getting to perform with some of our favorite players. The party traditionally becomes somewhat of a 'jam session'. Tonight, the stage would welcome such greats as Chuz Alfred's Swing Band, the fantastic keyboard work of Bob Mooney, Chad Rager's Jazz-Rock-Fusion Band, Donnie Wilson, Greg Herman, The Best Funky Blues by The Host Band, The Columbus Jets, of course Billy Bostwick's Fo-Pa Band playing Cajun style rhythmn and blues rock, and especially, Al Roop's All-Star Band.

The real show-stopper began, however, when two people helped an elderly gentleman to the stage. He was very frail looking. Friends helped him to a chair set in the middle of the stage. His wife then handed him his alto saxophone.

Looking as though he might not have enough lung capacity to blow a note, he shared a few words with Chuz Alfred - who accompanied him - and they were off and cook-

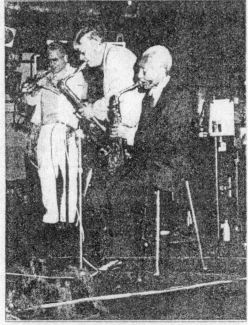

submitted

George James, former alto saxophone player for Louis Armstrong, joined local musicians at the Roop Brother's Annual Party.

ing! He had enough energy and excitement to knock your socks

off involuntarily!

After a burning start, his next song was so soft and sensitive it could bring a tear to your eye.

The main point is ... this guy could blow a mean horn and didn't want to quit. After a few songs that had *all* received standing ovations from the crowd, two people helped him off the stage and back to his seat. There his wife lovingly put his sax away and the two of them settled back to enjoy the rest of the show. Of course, I imagine he enjoyed himself after stealing everyone else's thunder. Which is exactly what George James, former alto sax player for Louis Armstrong, did - and, I might add, to the immense pleasure of all of us present.

This year's jam had turned into a great bash with music that hit all ages, which brings me to another point: I've seen great young players come into a jam that are just

My Brother-in Law, Phil, and my sister Ginny and their kids

***

THE BAR OWNING YEARS ...

The Roop Brothers Backyard parties went on for twenty-nine great years. There was a few years break; I had moved to Delaware and before you know it I ended up buying Roop Brothers Bar, the old Army Navy Club from my friend Ken Wiese, a very good man. He worked on me to buy it for two years.

I got it and turned it into Roops in 2006, the first of 2006, and a few people told me, they said, "You know, you boys talked about but you never did the thirtieth party." We were going to do thirty and retire the backyard parties before somebody got hurt or something. It was nice to hear somebody say, "Well now you have done the thirtieth party, you bought Roop's."

A lot of the same bands at the parties were playing at Roop Brothers Bar in downtown Delaware, which is still a great place. They said that's like party number thirty; it just didn't stop, and it's still going on. If that's so, that that was party number thirty. We're up to party number forty-one now I guess. That's quite some time.

What band would people be surprised that I like? I think Prince was awful damn good. The band Slightly Stupid is also. They have a good groove as do Cameo, Whispers, and Keith Urban.

We had a lot of fun with the Willie Pooch Band, T-Bone and Cheeseburger. Donnie Hops from Detroit, Willie and myself at a place called the Blue Note on Carson Street. Carson has about eighty bars on it. It's a great street on the southside of Pittsburgh.

The Blue Note is part of Permanny Brothers, the famous sandwiches where whatever sandwich you get has French fries on it, loaded up. One time I was walking down the road there, just wandering down Carson Street; and they were having a big party. There's some colleges kids, and even guys in their sixties and seventies, with weird colored plumes coming out of their hats, and instead of grey hair, their hair was turquoise or purple, pretty wild, and a variety of people and artsy stuff. They were selling wind chimes along the street.

Some bars had a one-piece band, or two or four or five piece bands, and down this one alley, it was a dead end street to the river; they had beer stands, and the band was just kicking ass. They were really good. So I walked down there, I was getting closer to the band and, my god, it was Edgar Winter, playing on an outside stage on this little dead end road by the river at Carson Street, free.

Me and Ed went over with the band and took my wife and mom along. We checked out the early band, it was Chizmo Charles and Dave Bell. I guess they had been at this bar for over ten years on Saturdays. We played ten p.m. to two a.m. This little place has a band every night of the week, three on Saturday, and two on Sunday with their wild, church service jam. The bandstand is over the bathrooms in the back of the place, up a staircase. We had to carry the B-3 up there; it overlooks a bar that probably seats seventy, and then it is just a stand-up rail all the way around the perimeter. And they pack it all the time.

Ed heard about three songs, and this guy was just tearing up some Santana, and Chizmo Charles was coming down the staircase and went behind the bar and was leaning over the rail singing a song to mom and putting on a good show, and Ed said, "I think you boys got your work cut out for you following these bad asses."

We ended up playing over there quite a bit and always had a good time. When we first got there, instead of going straight to the hotel, as usual, Ed had a great idea. We had been driving for four hours or something, and we've been chitchatting with Mom, and we needed a drink. We pulled in down at the bar. We got a seat at the bar, got Mom her seven and seven, and me and Ed got beers, a couple of Buds. And he said, "Well, what do you think Al? Tequila or Jager?"

And Mom said, "Oh, you boys, I just hate those dumb shots you drink. Why don't you get a nice drink, something mixed with something instead of drinking that old stuff straight."

So Ed said, "Okay, two Buds and two Jim Beam Manhattans up."

And Mom said, "There, that's better." The bartender was scratching her

The Bluenote in Pittsburgh where Mom is serenaded by Chismo Charles

head like what the hell just happened. It's a Manhattan, and Mom loved those so that was good in her book, so we drank Manhattans instead of Cuervo or Jager, and Mom was tickled.

We went back to the hotel where they had a really nice atrium bar, a big kind of sprawling space with a ceiling that went up two floors. They had this real cool water fountain; it came out of the ceiling a couple of floors up. I imagine it was maybe ten foot by ten foot, a big square wall of water that came down into a pond. It sounded good, and it looked beautiful. The bartender came over, and we were talking to him and looking straight past him at this enormous wall of water coming out of the ceiling and Ed say, "Boy, you got quite the leak."

He got us our drinks, and he must have gone over to the house phone and called maintenance. Because all of a sudden a guy shows up, in a green maintenance work suit, and he says, "Excuse me you guys. It was reported to me that you detected a bad leak in our ceiling."

Ed said, "Yeah, my god, look how much water is coming out of that ceiling. That's a hell of a leak."

The guy said, "Is that what you were talking about?"

Ed said, "Yeah." They didn't realize Ed's dry humor.

Probably the worst time we played over there I left my cymbal bag at home, so I didn't have any cymbals whatsoever. No high-hat cymbals, no cymbals, no extra sticks. We were all set up about ready to play and poor T-Bone was probably freaking out. We went on a mission talking to everybody and somebody said they could get some. I said, "Well I'll give you fifty bucks if you could turn up a set of high head cymbals and a pair of sticks."

So they go looking, and they came back with these about worn out tooth-picks. A lot of times I could go through a couple sets of sticks a night, so I had to be careful with these. I wrapped some duct tape on them to give them a little more strength. And the high hat cymbals that you work with your left foot, if I pushed down too hard on my left foot, they almost collapsed backwards against each other. But somehow it made me play simpler, just keeping it in the pocket.

***

OF ALL MY TRAVELS around the country, there were a number of places I liked. I discovered Treasure Island in Florida. Treasure Island is really part of St. Pete Beach/ St Pete area. There is a strand that starts about eight miles north at Clearwater Beach, then it goes down through Indian Shores, Indian Rocks, Madeira Beach, to Treasure Island, to St. Pete Beach.

Treasure Island is two miles long and really only street wide with the gulf on one side and the intercostal on the backside. The Boca Sitka Bay is part of the intercostal. To the east of that is the Tampa Bay. It's about twenty miles over water to Treasure Island, starting north at John's Pass to the intercostal, and Blind Pass to the south..

At Treasure Island, you still think it's the seventies. It's not a tourist trap,

there are no go cart tracks or golf cars. Just good restaurants, good neighborhood bars, and patios. They're really not interested in tourists. Sometimes I would be sitting at my favorite place Lana's, and they'll say something to me like, "Oh, those damn tourists, not you Roop, you're one of us. You're a towny." I've been going there since 1985 and so had my brother. We discovered it about a year apart. Clearwater and St. Pete Beach are expensive, but we just liked Treasure Island, which has about fifteen great bars and restaurants located downtown that are priced like Roop Brothers, and they take good care of you. Every one of them opens at eight in the morning and stays open until two thirty in the morning.

And one thing we learned over the years is you never want to cross the Skyway Bridge to Sarasota or any of those areas south. There's just fancy shopping centers, yacht clubs and stuffy, terribly expensive places, and it just

gets more expensive the farther you go because you end up in Naples.

The other thing is with the intercoastal and the Boca Sitka Bay and the Tampa Bay behind you, in the Treasure Island area you never see a mosquito because it is too windy. I think that somebody said if it's seven miles an hour or more it's too windy for some bugs. I have never been bitten by a mosquito in Treasure Island. You go across that Skyway Bridge to Sarasota, and it's much more humid because there is no air movement. There is no water on the other side to keep air moving and the bugs away.

It can be ninety degrees and feel like it's eighty with a great breeze in Treasure Island. Go across the Skyway Bridge to Sarasota and south, it's humid as hell, hot, muggy and plenty of bugs.

Speaking of the Boca Sika Bay that's right behind Treasure Island, if you are on the east side of Treasure Island looking at the west side of St. Pete, you can see the indoor pool and dock from the movie Cocoon.

They're all huge houses there on west side of St. Petersburg. It's by far

Legend's - Cappy & Whity

the best two miles I've found, the town and the white powder beach, with hotels like the T-Bird and the Belmar. About a block south of the hotels are some cabins called the "Sea Horse Cottages," right across the street from the grocery store, that's handy, and Walgreens is a liquor store.

These little cabins are like your own house on the beach. We like cabin 5, it's a single room cabin, a queen size bed, a couch and a chair and new kitchen, all knotty pine interior, built in the late fifties. Some people worry about storms, but we never have. Those little cabins have been there since 1956 or 1957.

You get up in the morning and open probably seven or eight windows, and you are looking right at the beach. There are some sea oats that block a couple of the windows, nice for shade. To this day, still, you can go there for a week for five hundred bucks, about six hundred with tax for seven nights, and they don't care if we take our dogs.

We take a couple little dogs, the Doxies. In the evening when it cools down, I walk them up to the Belmar and listen to the band while sitting out on the patio. Then I take the dogs back and walk back down to Ricky T's.

Our favorite bar is Lana's. She also owns the R Bar where a couple of nights a week they have all you can eat snow crab for nineteen bucks. One

night is all you can eat prime rib. A buddy of mine Steve Mills went down and he said, "Usually things aren't like people describe them, but you said it's like a small surfer village out of the seventies. You weren't kidding. It's exactly what it's like."

There was a mom and pop hotel we liked, the Harbor Inn. A gal named Sheila owned it. It was L-shaped, two floors, probably sixteen units or so.

It had a nice pool in the back, right on the intercoastal. You could stand in the pool have a drink and watch the yachts go by. Occasionally we would borrow Sheila's fishing poles, fish and have a good time. She had a good old

golden retriever, Goldie. Karyol and I always liked to get the room on the corner, right above the pool on the second floor. It had a good view of the Boca Ciega Bay and the intercoastal. We would always leave our door open.

There was a great breeze all of the time and that way Goldie could come in and visit us. I always took a box of Milk Bones with us for Goldie.

Probably Karyol's favorite story about what a dumbass I can be is I would always go see my buddies in the morning at nine or ten until noon or so for our coffee club at Lana's; and a few beers and few Jagers with Timmy, Cappy and Tommy the bartender or Jeanne. I had a little buzz. I came back and flopped down in my rocker. Karyol was watching TV, and Goldie came in for a visit. Karyol was men-

tioning, "You look awfully comfortable this early."

I said, "Yes, I sure am." I gave Goldie some Milk Bones, and I was rubbing her belly and I said, "Well, I think since we were here last, Goldie has had puppies." I was fondling a very, very large teet.

She said, "That's funny. Al, you buzzhead, didn't you know Goldie is a boy?" I wasn't fondling a teet; she was sitting there watching me massage his winkie. Oops!

Another great night we had there, Caddy's had real bands. We loved going over there for lunch. We noticed the marquee said, "Tonight, of Blues Brothers' Fame, the Downchild Blues Band." I thought, "Oh man, I love that band."

In the original Blues Brothers' movie, about half the stuff they did was the Downchild Blues Band. It was Ackroyd's favorite band from Canada; he turned Belushi on to them. "Flip, Flop and Fly" was theirs. "Rubber Biscuit" was theirs, and one of my favorites "Shot Gun Blues."

So, I went back that night. I wasn't going to miss a band like that. I sat down at the bar talking to their manager, a nice older gentleman who was walking around selling their CDs. I asked him which one I should buy. I told him that I played with Willie Pooch. He asked if I had a CD that we could trade. We did.

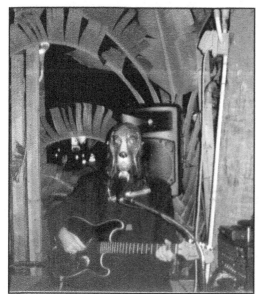

He said, "I'll get Donnie over here; it's his band."

Donnie and I were about the same kind of guy, probably about the same age. We sat down at the bar, and the girl came up, a beautiful bartender, and said, "Oh, I know you; you're in the band."

He said, "Yes, I am."

She said, "Well, your booze is free."

He said, "Oh great, I will

have a vodka and tonic."

And he said, "Al, what are you having?"

And I said, "Oh, I'll have a vodka and cranberry."

He said, "Dear, he's in a band too. Isn't his free?"

She thought about it for a minute and said, to our surprise, "Well, yeah, I guess his should be free too." We couldn't believe it. She went to get our drinks; we had several more, and she never did charge us. Some good moments at Treasure Island.

I remembered one of the beauties of downtown. We would stay at the Thunderbird a lot, and go out the side entrance off the patio to a sidewalk where we could jaywalk over to Ricky T's.

We would sit on the front patio bar of Ricky T's for awhile and watch the world go by, hear a guitar player, cut through the inside of Ricky T's to the

back patio that's under a roof and see what was going on.

Then we would go out the back patio down the alley that ran to the back entrance of Lana's Lounge. We'd go in for a bit then go out the front

Karyol, Willie and George

door of Lana's, and cross the street over to the R Bar to see what was going on over there.

Maybe we get a sandwich; then we would go back to Lana's in the front, go out the back of Lana's and go in the back door of the VIP, a little Mexican bar with great food.

Out the front of the VIP, and we'd go next door to Ricky's again, or jaywalk again back to the T-Bird's Tiki bar and next door to Sloppy Joe's at the Billmar. That was a good loop of going in front doors and out backdoors and continuing from one place to another, a Roop Loop. They are all in one block. Ed would say, it's time to get a margarita at the Tiki Bar, and he would say, "We better do laundry."

I would say, "Yeah, I guess you are right."

So we would go over to the Jacuzzi, sit down, and that was "washing our clothes." Then with the bubbles and the chlorine, Ed would say, "Well, time to agitate." So we would both bounce up and down, a half a dozen times to agitate our laundry. Get cleaned-up real good. Sit back and finish our drinks.

Then it was time to get back over to the bar. So he would say, "Time to

rinse." We would dive into the swimming pool and swim to the other end where we would climb out and take bar stools, then we would dry off sitting at the bar. That's how we did "laundry" every day.

Lana always knew I didn't wear shoes, and it would just drive her crazy sometimes, so when we went back over later I went in Walgreens and got some flippers. When we go over there she said, "Goddamnit, I know I don't even have to look, you don't have shoes on."

I said, "Yes, I do."

I had my legs crossed so she could see. She got up on her tiptoes and looked over the bar and said, "You're a dumbass. What the fuck's wrong with you Roop?" She had a drink with us, and life was good. She was from

Mansfield, Ohio.

Her place has always taken care of us, as soon as we would go in the door

at Lana's Lounge, we would always stop in there before the hotel,. Timmy or Jeanne would say, "Oh, my god, when did you get in town?"

A couple of our buddies from Canada were always there in the morning for coffee club. They would say, "Well, get a bucket ready to do a safety check of the island, and show us what's new or what they have screwed up." She would get a bucket of beers, all iced down for us, and we would end up stuck in a caddy or in the front seat of a pick-up truck. We would go from one end of

the island to the other and see what was going on.

That was always a tradition, and another tradition was when Timmy and the morning gang got there, and Devino and Joe; it was customary to play the Willie Pooch Tour album.

After hanging out back at the hotel, we walked back over to Ricky T's. The little front bar had a couple of TVs; it was right on the sidewalk, so you could watch the cars, enjoy the air at midnight, and it was beautiful. I'm sure we watched all of the evening shows or an old movie until two in the morning.

It just couldn't get any better than sitting outside right by the street, right across from the water. One time Casablanca was on. It was the first time that I ever got to see the whole thing.

***

THE BAR DAYS

Back here at home, before I bought the bar, I was hanging out at a place in Delaware called the Finish Line. I bought a house up there, and I worked on redoing it all summer, and went to the Finish Line to eat a lot. An old friend from the Gathering Inn Mike Palmer owned it.

One night, it was just me and him. We were on one corner, the bartender on the other. She had pop, water, her phone, chips and a book. Mike told me he was about to give up and close the place come the first of the year. He asked if I had any ideas to tell him.

I played nights; and my remodeling was done, so I said I would open week-days and build a good cocktail hour. He thought that was great, and said that I could do anything I wanted, like it was my place. He also said you can bring your band in a night a week if you want. Or I'll just close it. Mike asked the bartender for a couple beers, and she didn't even look up from her book. Mike, in his deep voice said, "See she won't even wait on me, and I own the damn place."

I said I'd like to get Rocky a Jager. Rocky was our buddy the cook. She said, "I don't think he'll want one."

Mike in that great voice says, "Oh, I think you're wrong there!"

I said, "I'll take the job." Mike said we have to wait three or four weeks to get past Christmas, so maybe mid January. Our buddy Joe Cardwell had put the kitchen in and was the first chef. Mike, Joe and myself were quite a team. Those stories would take another book.

I ended up bartending during the day and playing there on Wednesday nights with the Barrel House Blues Band. We later added Saturday bands, including Willie Pooch. When we first told people we were going to have a blues band there, they all said maybe one night a month, but it will not work. This is a dance street they said. I think they meant hip hop or country or something.

But they thought me and Mike were nuts. It went so well we added Friday. I had some friends at Vinny's Pub in Arlington, Kreis, Crump & Ross. They had been there for at least ten years on Thursdays. I had to tell Mike it was going to cost a hundred bucks more than the other five piece bands we were using. It didn't make sense to him for a trio. Mike was the best; that's why it worked, and he said I told you in the beginning I'm with you; get them in here. After their first night there Mike said, "That's the best hundred bucks I ever spent."

Price can never go by the size of a band. To this day, Kreis, Crump and Ross have played every Friday night in Delaware at Roop's. At Roop's they dropped Crump and picked up a kickass drummer Sammy Hooff, making it Kreis, Ross and Hooff. Everyone loved the music, the sunken bar, the fat rolly chairs, strip steaks and wings.

One special night we had the Mojo Kings and Barrel House play together,

Kreis, Crump & Ross

all of us. That's when I think you could say, and rest is history. Music in Delaware was kicking ass. Nobody likes a big place, or a cover charge, so this was it. I sure thank Mike for trusting me; he's a man of his word.

I met another musician from Delaware, Rick Bending, at the Finish Line. We got to shooting the shit. He had been talking about being in Denver; and I asked, "Did you ever find a town up above Denver, about a half-hour, forty minutes, called Evergreen?"

He said, "Oh yeah, hell yeah. I loved Evergreen. I went there a lot." When I was living out there, I did too to keep my sanity.

I don't know who said it first, maybe Rick said, "Did you ever discover Little Bear?" It's a neat old rustic wood bar, and it specialized in dark beer and buffalo burgers?"

I said, "Yes, it might have been at that time the only bar in Evergreen." It's an artsy little town for fishing for rainbow trout and candle shops, and maybe a couple of t-shirt shops and this bar, Little Bear. It has panties and bras on the walls, and old beer signs and dollar bills stuck to the wall. It was a pretty cozy old place. I said, "When I went there, there was a great band called Timothy P. and Rural Route 3."

He said, "Oh, my god, little Timmy P. and Rural Route 3?" Timmy was a big sonofabitch with bib overalls and no shirt under it. He would hold the straps of his bibs, and they would lower the American flag behind him when he was singing a certain song. I couldn't believe it.

In the seventies, I got his record album called Utah Moon featuring the old Rocky Mountain two-step. By the time Rick was there, that was in 1998, and he had bought his CD; and old Timothy P was still there. And as it turns out, I guess he is still there to this day. I remember talking to him once, and he seemed like a good old boy. I asked him, "Have you lived out here all of your life?"

All of the sudden his old good old boy accent was gone and he said, "Oh shit, no man, I'm from Chicago. I just came out here. I love this place. I have been here like four or five years or whatever." That was in 1974. When

Rick was there that was in 1998, and he was still there. He has found him a good gig.

***

TALKING WITH OTHER MUSICIANS like Rick Bending is interesting. We would talk about things you have to do if you want to be a professional musician. You know, travel is one, and sometimes you are low on money, or out. When you put a new band together, that's a drawback; but when it is in your blood, and you want to do it for a living, it's discouraging when you don't get to play what you like all of the time or even at all.

I'm always amazed when a band gets together and they go, "Oh, we're only going to do this stuff," or "We're only going to do original stuff." Boy, that doesn't work well, even as much as I hated some of the show tunes we had to play, or how much can you do "Jeremiah Was a Bullfrog" night after night, after night, month after month, year after year, or somebody saying, "Do big wheel on the river."

"You mean 'Proud Mary?' We'll sure play it for ya."

You just have to love your job for what it is, whatever song or whatever style. So many times you just had to act like you loved playing "Midnight Blue" or "Midnight at the Oasis" or songs from "Lady Sings the Blues" or a "Star is Born." Couldn't you just puke? What the hell; even if it sucks, you had to play it; and if you just tried to play it good, it made it easier. You had to play all of it with your heart and soul and play it with finesse, and play it with balls and power, whatever the song took. You got to take the good with the bad.

I was working with one band at the Sangria North in Columbus, and George Benson had just come out with "This Masquerade." I thought what a cool song that is. But the next song the band wanted to learn because it was a top forty hit was Tavares disco shit called "Heaven Must be Missing an Angel." Oh, I just hated that repetitive disco beat, but again, you have to do it. Sometimes you can put a little wrinkle to it, a little more funk or something and make it tolerable.

There are other fun things to help get through the nights when you are doing it all the time. Like I told you earlier, watching food and beverage managers make assholes out of themselves, bitching at staff or putting their hands over their ears, motioning for us to turn down. The uncoordinated dancers that if you spotted them, hell, you just about lost a beat and had to re-coup.

There were some other fun things within the band. You know, being the drummer, I usually sat right behind the singer; well, I always did. Billy Simpson, he would reach down and get his glass of Jim Beam, take a sip, and he would always turn around and look at me like, "How about a sip?"

Once I saw him coming toward me, reaching his arm over the top of my drums. I knew I either had to take a sip or wear it, so I would take a sip, and he would toast me, and the song would go on. I could tell you if Billy had BBQ or Taco's before he came to work. Sometimes he would back up to my drums, damn. I just about had all of Willie Pooch's leg moves down after sitting behind him off and on for thirty-five years.

One day, we were playing at this super club, and the owner would come out of the double-doors, where they came out of the kitchen. They were only for coming out with the trays, large trays for dinner. He would come out in his tuxedo and just get outside the doors where they would shut behind him, and then I think he would back up about a step.

This one girl came through and plowed through the doors. He was so pissed because he tumbled to his knees, and he punched her. Somehow she salvaged the tray. We thought it was B.S. because she got fired. He was standing in front of the out door, and she was coming out of the door like you are supposed to. We don't know if he got charged for hitting her.

Another time we were shocked. It probably wasn't the first time he ever did it to somebody, but a lot of the tunes you do in show clubs have big build-ups in them, dramatic builds where the instrumentation and the singer are reaching a peak.

Here again, a douche food and beverage manager would come out just in time to hear that it was too damn loud, but really the people were feeling the dynamics of the song, and they weren't upset. It was going to get quieter very soon, but of course, he made a quick judgment and in the middle of this beautiful build up, and he just comes up and turns the mains down, the whole main sound system, so that turns everything down.

What a slap in the face to a singer that has worked her ass off to build this song up to give you goose bumps and make you feel the moment. It's like pulling the rug out from under your feet.

Another great day of music was Roop Brothers Bar entry in the Delaware Christmas Parade with a band. I knew it was going to be my last, not the bar's last, so go big. It was big people said, "What are you going to do next year? Get a Boeing 707 and takes the wings off of it and make it a float, because of the size of our entry?"

My buddy, Pat Cashman had just found an old restored Kenworth, conventional long-nose semi tractor with a long double sleeper, big chrome stacks, chrome everything. It was a forty-foot long truck with a forty-foot flatbed trailer restored to go behind it. It was definitely very big to get through a city street.

If it wasn't for a great driver like Pat Paykoff, it could have been pretty hard to get it out to the parade route. But it was a great theme, and we wanted to go all out.

The theme of the parade was *Toy Story*, for this beautiful, rare old semi.
With white shoe polish we lettered down the sleeper in big letters the word
"Tonka," the Tonka toy logo, like it was a big toy. We laid it out for Christmas
with lights, garland and everything. We borrowed from Jimmy and Ryan Gill's,
at Chesrown, a new SS Camaro convertible, and we blew up "Hot Wheels"
logos to put on the side of it like it was a big toy.

All the guys from the Christmas breakfast at the hardware decided to ride
in it, John Freeman, Pat Cashman, Jed Flahive, and myself. With all the big
toys was a John Deere tractor, oversized toys and oversized boxes wrapped
up. My niece's son, Owen was our child enjoying the oversized toys on the
float for Christmas. Poor guy probably thought we were nuts.

We had to have a live band, so it was Delyn Christian and the Fret Shop
Band with their big upright bass, such good music. So we had the Camaro,
big Hot Wheels, and we had Owen and the toys and the live band like *Toy
Soldier's*, and this big Tonka toy truck, of course, on the back of the float it
said - "Our Toy Story."

It felt like it was twenty below zero the day of the parade. I bet it wasn't over twenty degrees, but it was just colder than hell. We were going down the parade route, and these poor guys playing suffered, especially DeLen playing guitar, the guy playing upright bass, and the other guitar player because his hands always hurt anyway, as he was always spraying them with some kind of lacquer to coat them.

But the band sounded great, and my buddy Jerry Blenn was running down the street keeping the PA dialed in just right. That was quite the *Toy Story*.

We didn't get far before Jed, sitting in the driver's seat said, "Ah, this car's got gas in it. Shit, I'm going to start it and get some heat. It's too damn cold." So we were running the Camaro. Boy, what a lot of room for things to go wrong, but we got the truck down the street, and the Camaro didn't fall off.

Jed said, "Damn, every time the truck goes around a corner, with the engine running," he said; "I keep steering the damn Camaro." We had already decided that even though it was colder than hell we would get to the end of the parade, then double-back.

We told Vasili that we would come by Bun's Restaurant and do a half-hour show on this big semi in front of his patio, where he opened the doors. Vasili bought the band dinner since they froze their butts off for us. They later played at Roop's that night, and it was quite the time.

***

OK, I GOT SIDETRACKED, back to the Finish Line, what a place it was. It was the first of 2004 when I started. Nobody could believe how good blues bands were doing at the Finish Line on a street that was mixed up musically.

For a short time there was a bar across the street called Club Impact dance bar; it was later called Manhattans, and now, thank god, 1808. Josh at 1808 is a good friend, and he helped me with some good bar ideas and good beer.

Also for a short time MiCerrito was Hencock wing bar. Bun's had no patio yet, and a very small bar. It's hard to believe how much Winter Street has changed.

Mike wanted to sell the building the Finish Line was in. The first of 2006 I bought the Army Navy Club on Union Street. There was no 1808 American Bistro, no MiCerrito's or Veritas, no Staas Brewery, no Choffey's, no Pat's Endaangered species, no four season patio at Bun's, and none of the theatres lights worked out front. All of the bars across from the Finish Line were closed. There was no Wooland Cigar, Old Bag of Nails just opened, and there was no Son of Thurman, no Restoration Brew Worx, J Gumbo, Barley Hopsters, Vito's Wine, Amatto's Wood Fired, Solar Saloon, Typhoon, 12 West San Diego style, or Oppa.

Kenny had tried to get me to buy the Army Navy for a year. I really enjoyed being around him. He reminded me of a younger version of my grandpa in a way.

He said, "Why don't you think about buying this?" It was a little freestanding building, seventeen hundred square feet. "It's on the City parking lot with great parking, and I'll make the price right for you."

Others tried to get it. He said, "I won't sell it to them because it will end up closed; they will screw up everything. You did a nice job at the Finish Line. You are the only person who I want to have it. You and your wife will have a little bit of retirement, something for down the road since you both have been self-employed."

I thought about it and thought about it, and one day I wrote a personal check. I probably had fifty bucks in my checking account, but I wrote him a personal check for five grand less than he wanted for it.

He poured me a shot and he just smiled, folded it up, put it in his top pocket. And he said, "That will work. Whenever you make it good down the road is fine with me. A handshake is good, just tell me when I can get the hell out of here."

That was about a week before Christmas, I think. I said, "About the first of February?" I wanted to get some neon signs together and get all of the supplies and lighting, a jukebox, everything lined up. I wanted to open it on February 1, 2006; that was on a Wednesday. It gave time for me and buddies to remodel the inside, and change the signs.

Kenny came to the grand-opening and just loved it. The band kicked ass, and the place looked good.

He said, "This is what I thought you would do with it." The next day he came in and he said, "Boy that was fun last night. The place was great." He passed away that evening. So my first Friday was a wake for my good friend Kenny Wiese, who I believe was 79 years old.

The family said, "Well, he waited over a year for you to buy the damn thing; apparently that's all he wanted."

I was so anxious to get it open that day and worried about stuff, again my brother's great sense of humor came through. He was a real good artist. He made a sign and had it hanging by the door so when I came in this big sign said, "Welcome to Al's Country Bunker."

The rest is history. It went for nine and a half years as Roop Brothers,

named after our backyard parties. Later that year Mike sold the Finish Line. Roop Brothers got the Friday band Kreis, Krump and Ross, and The MoJo Kings played every Wednesday. A tremendous single act, Bobby Lloyd did an open mic night and hosted it every Thursday to this day, about ten years.

A couple of years later there was Ski High karaoke, something I swore I would never have in a bar, but Scott and Heidi do a great job with it, and

A couple of songs written for me by Dickie Jackson

SHIT'S OVER   words & music by:
                                      Dickie Jackson 12/03/08

Oh, how well I do remember, was the third week of September.
This Sunday night was gonna be just great!
Me and Al had planned a show that would let those people know
We could rock this town and really flood the gates.

It was Barrel House and us, and we had put up quite a fuss
to convince those folks that we could pack 'em in.
so when those horses ran their run, we were keyed up for our fun.
Just about that time here came that big ole' wind.

That day Big Ike came into town, and it blew that big tent down
And the sheriff said "boys, ya'll get outta here."
Then, ole' Jim Beam Al and me took some Quervo, and went to pee,
But ole' Ike had blown that Porta-Potti down!

Shit's over, guess we were not meant to play.
Shit's over, we'll just drink the night away.
Old snob nob has just crashed, Nathan's snare drum's in the trash.
Do not show us to the gate, we don't want to evacuate!
We got whiskey and tequila, this is all we really needed-
Shit's over.

Tag:
Yea, we were gonna knock 'em dead, we got "blown away" instead,
If you wanna make a bet, bet we could blame this all on Sweat!
Shit's over!---------------don't call us next year!!!!!!

Dickie Jackson (signature)

Written 01/23/09 in honor of Jug week concert at the Delaware County Fair
featuring, *Double Barrel, The Barrel House Blues Band, and The Country Sunshine
Band.* The concert was canceled due to hurricane Ike hitting Delaware and the entire
fair grounds was evacuated.(except for Jim, Jose', Al & me)!

CARS, AND BARS, GUITARS, AND FRIENDS

words & music by:
Dick Jackson 11/15/06

Here's a little tune I just threw together
While sittin' in my truck in this November weather.
It's just a little ditty 'bout some odds and ends,
Like cars, and bars, guitars and friends.

Now, when it comes to cars, well, I've had many.
I even had a Cadillac limo, that I named *Lenny*.
I've had Corvettes, and Chevettes, I been a lucky feller,
And most of the time they was colored yeller!

I'll tell ya folks, I've got guitars galore!
I even got some from *Big Daddy's* store.
My wife, Cathy says I can't have no more!
But that's another story, altogether.

Which, finally, brings us to bars and friends.
And that's just about where my story ends.
I can sum it all up in one fowl swoop-
It's all about this place called *ROOP'S*

There's Al, of course, he's friendly, he's never been a snob.
But that fucker's had at least a hundred jobs!
He can run a bar, drive a limo car, and even play the drums.
Oh yea, there's Paul Yokum, he ain't got no thumb!!

You know we sit here all day, that's why we look so pale,
Of course I shouldn't say that about our old buddy, Dale.
You can get good whiskey, and cold Budwieser beer,
And drink it all down with Homer, and Roger Keyser near.

Yep, the atmosphere at *ROOP'S* is always fine.
Just ask St'Claire, if he can stop guzzlin' that wine!
And good old Bea, she's just as sweet as she seems,
But that crazy bitch puts diet pop in her glass of *Jim Beam!!*

Well, there's my story, 'bout cars, bars, guitars, and friends.
I'll bet you're glad this thing's about to end.
But then again you can't be too picky,
Here you sit, again, listenin' to this shit by Dickie!!! Yo Dee Lay Eeeeeee!!!

Written November 15th for the opening of Al, and Ed's *Roop Bros.* bar.
I was so proud that Al finally had a career! Good Luck, Budd!!

Mark May Band with Soul Saytr Horns

are still there every Monday. I'm glad, and lucky I changed. Some of the other bands are Dolly Dagger; Vintage, a great classic rock band; and Rolly

Eliot Lewis from Hall & Oates

Gaumer and the Leftovers, named the Leftovers because it was Rolly from the Rolling Hams, Dicky Jackson of Country Sunshine, George McDonald from Barrel House, and myself. Now it's a larger band.

And our wild buddies, the Divide, Next of Kin, they are probably one of the only bands that really can nail Grand Funk Railroad. One of my favorite bands is Mark May. The Mark May Band featuring Soul Satyr horns; and with twin lead guitar players, few can do Allman Brothers "Whipping Post" or "Memory

Rick Calura, Pooch & Dave Workman

of Elizabeth Reed," like these guys can, and had one of the best drummers I have heard.

Mark was with Dicky Betts and Great Southern for over seven years. Also Burning Diesel, Terry Davidson and the Gears, Bobby Lloyd's band the Thirsty

Tommy, Jim Biersdorg, Pooch & Bostwick

Otis & Schwab

Kreis, Joe Crump & Ricky Hall

Travelers, Delyn Christian and the Mojo Kings, the Lucky Penny, Don Mc-
Cann, the Lane Brother's and Ora Conn were there to help.

We were lucky to have some special guys like Eliot Lewis, who was originally with the Average White Band, and for the last twelve years has been

Johny Mac's Soul

with Hall & Oates. He is also on Darryl Hall's TV show, a great music show called "Live from Darryl's House."

Another buddy that we loved who would come up from Texas is John DelToro Richardson, who played absolutely great, great Texas blues. Dave Workman who is now in California and works for Santana comes to town and battles it out with Rick Calura of the MoJo Kings on guitar, and there is no better guitar battle than that one. Also, the magic of Steven Kline.

From Cincinnati the Blues Merchants are pretty cool with a beautiful Irish gal as lead singer. The keyboard player was originally in a band called the "Lemon Pipers" that wrote the song "My Green Tambourine."

That goes back a ways, but he is a hell of a good guy. He has a cool Hammond organ, old school, not quite as big as a B-3, but similar. He bought it when John Mayall was touring in America and didn't want to ship it back over seas, so it's John Mayall's original Hammond in the Blues Merchants.

Another special guy that came to the bar a lot, and still does, is Buckeye Boys BBQ Big Dave. What musician doesn't love BBQ? One day I was going to sit in with the Friday guys; I loved to play a few with them. There was a young guy in cargo shorts and t-shirt, pretty kick-back looking, young. He

Chris of Dolly Dagger responsible for the book project

Dolly Dagger

was going up at the same time I was, and I thought, oh man, I was hoping to play with Randy Ross playing guitar, because he's playing Eric Clapton. Oh well, this will be fun anyway, play a few songs, and call it.

This young guy straps on a guitar, and he looked at the rest of us and said, "What about 'Born Under a Bad Sign,' everybody likes that one." I thought well, that's great shit, "Born Under a Bad Sign" and hell, he played great. I enjoyed working with him.

We got done playing, and I went up and got a beer. I saw him sitting in the back by the stage so I went back to thank him and tell him how great he was. It turns out he had been in Columbus at a hotel and asked somebody where he could go and sit in with a band and play a little bit. He was Darius Ruckers' guitar player, and they were in town. Someone knew about my bar, and said, "You could go up to Roop's in Delaware and play with some great guys up there. It's not very far away." It was a just a nice to meet him.

Around this time I was slowing down, occasionally I still played full nights with Rolly or somebody. By this time, it's hard to believe, I'd done sixteen straight years with the Barrel House Band and with Pooch, off and on for over thirty five years and with my friend Donnie Wilson and all of the bands I was in with Bob Mohney. It was great to have all of these kick-ass players come into little Roop Brothers' bar.

***

WE ALREADY TALKED about the worst gig, with the "Tie Me Kangaroo Down Sport" shit at the hotel in Dayton, but what's the best gig ever? That's got to be when we played at the Polaris Ampitheater. I lived on East Powell Road at the time, so I wasn't but a mile away from it.

Being on that billing was incredible. It was Jimmy Vaughan and the Fabulous Thunderbirds, Joe Cocker, Buddy Guy, and Willie Pooch. Willie and Buddy Guy were very, very good friends and that sure led to some fun days in Chicago at Legends. We sat backstage, me and Willie and Buddy. We had fried pork chops, fried potatoes and onions and peppers, and there was a great bartender who just kept the drinks coming.

I loved bullshitting with those two great guys, Pooch and Buddy. We got all greased up with eating pork chops with our fingers, one after another. They brought us more potatoes and more of whatever it was we were drinking, I don't know. It was Cavasia or something. What a gig!

It was probably around 2010, and we were going to do an extra special show to open the fair week for the Little Brown Jug Race in the big VIP tent. We were going to put together Dicky Jackson, the Country Sunshine band, along with the Barrel House Band and do a huge event with each of us doing a set and then coming back together. I suppose it would be about fifteen of us playing a big finale.

I think it was going to be one of the biggest events ever there, but that was the year the hurricane came through. The tent was probably a couple of hundred feet long, and it's huge on turn one of the track. They had bulldozers and dump trucks, everything roped to the tent, trying to hold it down in that terrible weather. It still looked like a serpent moving. Jerry Blinn was doing sound, and he had probably a thirty or forty channel snake going from the sound system, up through the top to where he was. The winds tore the snake in half.

We were at a campsite, just a couple of rows over from the tent with Dicky Jackson, Queen Automotive and Wes and Gena's Compound. We were waiting to see what was going with this show. Of course, they scrapped the show. They let us know that it wasn't going to happen. They were getting people out of the fairgrounds, because there was seventy mph winds; it was terrible.

So we were sitting there as they were herding people out. Apparently they didn't care if we left, and they let us stay. Dicky was playing guitar, and some other people were playing. I was playing my snare drum upside down like a banjo.

When they cancelled the show, Dicky said, "Well, Cathy, get the Tequila out of the freezer." So we had a few shots, and the wind got terrible. There was about a four unit port-a-potty setup by the tent, a fenced in area up on the turn, and this big port-a-potty blew over the fence and fell over the embankment down to the parking lot where the campers were.

Dicky looked at us and said, "Well, shit's over now." And he started singing a song that he wrote about that night, both of the bands and the shitter falling over the hill. About then a metal sign flew into the side of a camper. Dicky kept singing, "The shit's over now."

I remember I got home, and my poor Karyol said, "Did you ever think of calling?" I was at a loss for words. We were so busy writing music and singing because our big gig was scrubbed. I kind of missed the boat on that one, and just another screw up on my part.

***

AROUND THE SAME TIME Dicky Jackson's band Country Sunshine were having their thirty-fifth anniversary of being together. We all loved to do screw overs. This was probably the best of my life. Country Sunshine was at Roop's, and they had, I think his name is Skeeter Wolf, a well-known Nashville pedal steel player and Country Sunshine's whole band of great guys. The Boggs, all of them. They were playing, and they had a big banner up "35th Anniversary of Country Sunshine."

I happened to know that John Schwab was doing a private party up at the fairgrounds. So I called him and told him I wanted to get Dicky real bad. Schawb's party only went to about nine p.m., so he thought he would be able to be at the bar by quarter of ten or something. He said he would call me when he was in the parking lot with his whole band, McGuffey Lane.

So I get John Schwab's phone call that they are in the parking lot. I tell them to hang on for a minute. I take up five or ten bucks to Dicky and Country Sunshine, and I said, "A couple of people here wanted to hear some McGuffey Lane. Could you do 'Give Me That Green Country Mountain' or something?"

They said, "Sure," and started playing the McGuffey Lane song, and I opened the door and motioned Schwab to come in. Schwab comes in in his black suit and cowboy hat and stands right in front of Dicky, his pedal steel player in his black suit comes in and stands in front of their guy, Steve, Lane's bass player and so on. So McGuffey Lane is standing in front of Country Sunshine, and

John Schwab and McGuffy Lane take over mid-song from Dick Jackson and Country Sunshine.

McGuffy Lane takes over from Country Sunshine

Country Sunshine is doing their song, You could see Dicky sweating and just shitting a brick. McGuffey Lane just stood in front of them with their hands on their hips, just staring at them.

I'll tell you, in the bar you could hear a pin drop; it was beautiful. Schwab steps up on the stage and takes Dicky's mic, the other guys switch, Schwab starts singing "Give Me That Green...", and the energy in the room was just absolutely overwhelming. Damn it was good, and everyone was on their feet. If you weren't there that night, you missed one of the greatest nights in Delaware music history. I sure thank John Schwab for helping me orchestrate a good screw over.

***

IT'S PROBABLY CLOSE to the same time that Pooch was doing terrible. He had been in Doctors' Hospital for many, many months. Henry Banks, of Banks Market on London Road, wanted to do something for Willie, and I wanted to do something for Willie. Amvets 03 was the spot. Banks Market did all of the food, and we had a huge party. We were selling CDs and pictures of Willie. Other bands there were the MoJo Kings and Big Al and the Capital City Players. We had to have a wheelchair van to get Willie out of Doctors' West Hospital.

We had that lined up, thanks to Buffalo, and we got Pooch there. We broke him out of the hospital after months, with the hospital's Ok. He was only able to do a few songs with his band, the MoJo Kings. And his signature song, we got to all hear it one more time, "Rainy Night in Georgia." It was unbelievable that Pooch was able to do it, but he did.

Submitted

Singer Willie Pooch and drummer Al Roop are seen at the Polaris Amphitheater earlier this year where they appeared on the same bill as Joe Cocker, Buddy Guy, and the Thunderbirds.

We sent him back to Doctors' Hospital. On the way back I guess he asked to stop, that he would like to have some Colonel Sanders. We didn't see Pooch again, as he passed three days later. But it was so nice of Banks and the Amvets to throw that good party for him. Henry Banks is a great man.

***

SPEAKING OF THE GOOD PEOPLE in Delaware, Vasili Konstantindis at Bun's, my buddy, has helped me over the years I have been in Delaware. Years ago I was playing at the Brown Derby Restaurant on Morse Road, and I didn't

Vasili

know it was Vasili's place. Years down the road he ended up with Bun's Restaurant in Delaware, and that's when we got talking about his friends that I also knew, at the Whiskey Still and Fisherman's Wharf.

I couldn't believe that I worked for Vasili, and here all of these years later I run into him in Delaware. My buddy Jerry Blinn was in the band Black Leather

Touch. I use to see them in the seventies. We did van shows together, and I think I had seen his band in Dayton.

It turns out Jerry left the west side of Columbus and came to Delaware and Bun's. He has helped me with many music events and floats in Delaware. Sitting at Bun's several times I had a drink with a guy named Geb. He said he liked my bar Roops, and liked the bands, and we talked quite a bit.

Geb and Shirley said they would like to have us over sometime or meet at Bun's. I had been running into them for a couple of months. Geb gives me his card, and I see his full name on the card is Geb Kenny. Geb Kenny stuck out in my mind because my father worked with Geb Kenny. They were pioneers of plastic housewares, canisters, and stuff, from the mid-thirties to the mid-sixties. Dad worked with Geb Kenny, and they were very good friends. So I asked Geb who looks my age, what did your Dad do? He said he made plastic housewares.

I said, "Well, you are not going to believe what my dad did – he worked at Lusterware Columbus plastics."

He said, "Holy shit, you're Nate's kid." So here's Nate and Geb at over sixty, and our Dads would both have been pushing a hundred years old. We had never met, but both ended up in Delaware.

It's fun to have a toast to Geb and Nate. Vasili from the Brown Derby is in Delaware; Jerry Blinn from Black Leather Touch from the west side of Columbus is in Delaware; Geb from Columbus, and my buddy Jimmy Gill, who I mentioned earlier of Chesrown Chevy GMC; and Otis, lead singer of the Jets, came up from Columbus. It's something and what a small world!

***

WHAT BANDS WOULD I LIKE to be in right now? It's Bruno Mars, any band Chester Thompson would be playing a Hammond B3 in, or Here Come the Mummies.

***

ON SEPTEMBER 1, 2014, after negotiating for a few months, Josh and Micah bought Roop Brothers. It was time for me to move on. I had ten years in. It needed younger blood and younger ideas, a little more refreshing. It was time. They wanted to keep the name, but change it from Roop Brothers to just

Josh, Al & Micah

Roop's, which makes sense.

They wanted to respect me and my brother with the background that we had there. They wanted to keep the music legacy alive, book bands a year out like I did, add more craft and import beers, and have beer on tap. They wanted to add new A/C, new stage, a new JBL sound system, bigger TVs, and have music four to five nights a week. They enjoy visiting all the good spots in town like I did. I just couldn't have found better guys and gals to keep moving forward, and the legend lives on. I'm very proud of them.

***

AFTER OVER FORTY YEARS, I am sometimes asked who is a very special musician that has been a major influence on me? It's Eric Clapton. Eric Clapton brought us some of the most incredible music ever.

No one else can say they were in this number of the greatest bands in the world. Clapton had the Yardbirds, Blind Faith, and Derek and Dominos. I named one of my dogs after Derek and the Dominos' "Layla," a black Afghan. He was also with Bonnie & Delaney. One of the most incredible bands ever was Cream. The first band I was in played a lot of Cream, including the great song by Robert Johnson, "Crossroads." They had another one of my idol drummers, Ginger Baker. So hats off to Eric. Also Stevie Wonder and Greg Allman are special musicians to me.

***

YOU KNOW I JUST HOPE this book brings back some good memories of bands, songs, bar and nightclub memories. I hope it made you laugh a time or two. These events were from 1954 thru 2014. I'm sorry if I missed a good story you remember.

And I'm sorry for any musician or band I overlooked. My memory is about as good as my damn back. It's been well over a year that I have been adding to my notes, so many memories have come back that filled in between the original notes, and it has been a joy. My thanks to the guys that made my life as a musician work out - Don Beck, Gene Deffenbaugh, Donnie Wilson, Bob Mohney and Willie Pooch. They all took me under their wings when I was a kid.

***

THANKS TO THE FRIENDS, fans, bartenders, food servers, and fellow musicians, buddies that made forty years plus something special.

***

IT WOULD BE TERRIBLE if I didn't thank my favorite bartender, my wife Karyol, for putting up with me for thirty-three years. Like the song Andy sang in the Mojo Kings, "Your pinch paid off." All of the music, the stories and shit she has had to listen to.

And our son, Matt, a great

guy. I thank Matt for having a sense of humor like my brother; that's a special gift. To our doggies-George, Willy, Jay, Gracie, Daisy, Cats- Flo Ginny, Sammy, Sunny, and the crazy parrot- Tampa.

Matt and Al on Matt's 34th Birthday

***

WHAT DO I ENJOY DOING now that the band and bar years are behind me? Well, I love old TV shows on the antenna, out on the porch, well almost anything funny.

Karyol and I have discovered we like cruises, and we figured out how to do it to fit our unnormal life style. We like the eastern cruise on Holland America ships. We've done it five or six times, and we go for the boat, not really ports of call. We like walking around, inside, outside, eating whenever, sitting at the pool bar, or on the patio at our room, and then do it all again, and again.

We've got it down. We have breakfast delivered to the room at seven thirty every day with a full breakfast and apple Danish with extra, extra butter, a pot of coffee, and we sit out on the patio.

When we are at a new port, we hang out, let everyone wait in line to go ashore; then about ten, we go up by the pool and hang out, listen to music, enjoy the breeze, get a burger and fries, look out at the town we are docked at.

By three or four we take a break at the room and sit outside. Everyone gets back to the ship to get ready for dinner, and we go eat when they are all in their rooms. They go to dinner, and we bar hop and walk around.

When they hit the bars, we go back outside on the aft pool deck and watch the sunset or the ship's wake. We snack here or there the whole time. We check out the band at the B.B. King lounge at eight, and by eleven go to the room for TV, or go out on the patio and watch the water, and listen to the waves with a tall cocktail.

The next day the ship is docked some place different, and they call over the speakers for everyone to meet to go ashore at about nine, but we are still kicked back with coffee. Then we work our way to one of the pools. In sun or out of sun, is the biggest question. The music is playing, there are few people on the ship, and it's time for Margaritas; it's a bitch. We enjoy the view of St. Thomas, St. Martin or Puerto Rico.

The next morning we start it off with breakfast delivered to the room again. I think that's what we want to do for the rest of our lives once a year, sit on the patio of our room on a Holland America ship and watch the world go by.

***

I ENJOYED IT EVERY TIME I heard Willie Pooch introduce the band. He had a different way to introduce each person in the band. When it was my turn to be introduced he would say,

"Before him there was none and after him there ain't going be no more, Catfish, Al Roop on drums."

Thanks Pooch.

Willie always finished the night with, "I'm gonna plant you now and dig you later."

***

WAS IT ALL WORTH IT? You bet your ass it was.

The view I had of smiles, people having fun, talking to friends in a booth, dancing, and watching the band. Spotting regulars coming in and giving us a wave, I'd give them a nod or point my sticks at them. Sometimes a tray of shots came to the stage. You can tell who sent them when you saw a table of folks smiling holding their shots in the air. I was also lucky to watch some great solos on stage, and see the crowd clapping.

Wish You All The Best,

Al Roop

"… and I'm still playing my Dad's drum after all these years. It must be 75 years old …. way older than me!" - Al